The

GRAND OPTION

Gethsemani Studies
in Psychological and Religious Anthropology

ERNEST DANIEL CARRERE, O.C.S.O.
Series Editor

has been funded through a generous grant by
RICHARD C. COLTON, JR.

Also in the series:

Contemplation in a World of Action
Thomas Merton

Freud and Psychoanalysis
W. W. Meissner, S.J., M.D.

The
GRAND
OPTION

Personal Transformation
and a New Creation

BEATRICE BRUTEAU

University of Notre Dame Press
Notre Dame, Indiana

Manufactured in the United States of America

The chapters of this work originally appeared in the following publications:

Chapter 1 in *Cistercian Studies* 19:151–162 (1984).
Chapter 2 in *Anima* (Spring 1977) and *Cross Currents* 27:170–182 (1977).
Chapter 3 in *Cross Currents* 31:273–284 (1981).
Chapter 4 in *The Theosophist* (Sept. 1983), pp. 527–533 and (Oct. 1983),
    pp. 21–25.
Chapter 5 in *Cistercian Studies* 22:199–212 (1987).
Chapter 6 in *Anima* (Fall 1975).
Chapter 7 in *Cross Currents* 35:190–205 (1985).
Chapter 8 in *Cistercian Studies* 18:42–58 (1983).
Chapter 9 in *Who Do People Say I Am?* (Francis Eigo, ed.) Villanova , Pa.:
    Villanova University Press, 1980.

Library of Congress Cataloging-in-Publication Data
Bruteau, Beatrice, 1930–
    The grand option : personal transformation and a new creation / Beatrice
Bruteau.
        p.   cm. — (Gethsemani studies in psychological and religious
    anthropology)
    Includes bibliographical references.
    ISBN 0-268-01041-2 (alk. paper) — ISBN 0-268-010412-0 (pbk. : alk. paper)
        1. Spirituality—Catholic Chuch.   2. Consciousness—Religious aspects—
    Catholic Church.   3. Human evolution—Religious aspects—Catholic
    Church.   I. Title.   II. Series.
BX2350.65 .B78   2001
233—dc21

                                                                00-012456

∞ *This book was printed on acid-free paper.*

Contents

Editor's Preface

Beatrice Bruteau has been in dialogue with the monks of Gethsemani for over twenty years. With presentations to the community, conferences to our junior professed, and ongoing discussions with various monks, she has been a vitalizing and sapiential presence beyond her annual visits.

Always ahead of her time, Dr. Bruteau is a creative thinker whose integral vision is as powerful and inspiring as it is realistic and concrete. "A new way of seeing," Teilhard de Chardin has exclaimed, "combined with a new way of acting—that is what we need."* This is precisely what we are given in *The Grand Option*.

Ages ago I urged Dr. Bruteau to gather together in a single volume the talks and essays that had so animated those of us who regularly met with her. I'm grateful that other projects intervened, for we now have the opportunity to include these rich contributions in our series.

The essays are not only as dynamic and vital as in their first presentation, but our world has evolved—both positively and negatively—into readiness for Dr. Bruteau's convergent perspective and global insight.

Positively, the world that has been drawing together through the miracle of cable news for over two decades is now on the verge of realizing Teilhard's anticipation of an intercommunicating "noosphere" of human reflective energies embracing and "planetizing"

Activation of Energy, p. 295 (New York: Harcourt Brace Jovanovich, 1970).

the earth, as both satellite links and the internet profoundly unite us as a global, interconnected, wholistic community. At the same time, it is traumatically evident that a paleolithic tribalism, perhaps more than ever, is brutally rampant throughout our earth. It is precisely this riven world that can most urgently benefit from Dr. Bruteau's healing vision of communion consciousness transforming us from conflicted and conflicting individuals into open, sharing, interpenetrating persons of a new creation. This is a bold possibility whose reality depends on you and me.

"I know of scarcely anybody," Bede Griffiths has said, "who goes to the heart of reality as profoundly as Beatrice Bruteau does." I concur; and for this reason *The Grand Option* is the third volume of Gethsemani Studies. If earnestly engaged and put into practice, this work of philosophical, theological, and psychological anthropology has the power to initiate a psychic revolution.

Gethsemani Studies in Psychological and Religious Anthropology is a series of books that explores, through the twin perspectives of psychology and religion, the dynamics and depths of being fully human. An integrated or dialogical perspective is always anticipated in the works; nevertheless, a title favoring the religious standpoint may appear if it bears psychological ramifications, while a title devoted to psychological issues may appear if it is foundational or contributes to the integrated and humanizing dialogue.

This dialogue embraces the entire range of dynamic psychology, from Freud and Jung to Kohut and Lacan, with special predilection, perhaps, for the insights of psychoanalytic object relations theory, while the work of Kernberg, Spotnitz, and Searles, to name only three, offers the promise of equal enrichment.

Gethsemani Studies would have remained an impossibility without the presence of Dick Colton. Dick recognized in the earliest, most speculative discussions that the series represented a worthy project. His dedicated interest cut through the hesitation that impedes new endeavors, inspiring the involvement of all, while his generous grant underwriting the series enabled Notre Dame and the Abbey of Gethsemani to work concretely toward its realization.

Jeff Gainey of the University of Notre Dame Press immediately perceived the potential of such a series and has labored as a wonderful colleague to realize its possibilities. Barbara Hanrahan, director of the press, has brought a rich publishing experience as well as a delightful collegiality to our deliberations.

It is a pleasure to acknowledge anew Wendy McMillen's superlative book designs. Margaret Gloster's covers have been extraordinary creations. Ann Bromley and Juanita Dix have contributed magnificent skills; and it has been wonderful to work with and to rely upon the editorial expertise of Rebecca DeBoer, Ann Hoade, and executive editor Ann Rice. No mention of the staff would be complete without acknowledging my appreciation of and indebtedness to both Gina Bixler and Diane Schaut. I especially appreciate the response of Chris Catanzarite, newest member of the staff, to her early reading of the manuscript.

Richard and Janita Rawls, as wonderful friends and wise colleagues, were primary consultants at the threshold of the series who continue to provide faithful counsel.

Eleanor Ash bestowed essential help throughout our preparations for this volume, while John Shea was of great assistance at a crucial moment. Clair Mahinske, Paula Mahinske, Theresa Sandok and Brinton Lykes all generously contributed to the project. Most important, Elsa Kirk was indispensable.

ONE

Activating Human Energy
for the Grand Option

The question that preoccupied Teilhard de Chardin was the question that preoccupies most people: Do our lives have any ultimate meaning? Is the human caravan going anywhere? If the human phenomenon is only a cosmic coincidence, a minor if extravagant eddy in the great downstream rush of the universe from "big bang" to maximum entropy, then our lives as persons are futile. In fact, we are a contradiction, Teilhard feels, for we and our need to find our lives meaningful are products of this very cosmic development. Has the universe given birth to a desire that cannot be fulfilled? How is that possible?

On the other hand, how can the desire be fulfilled? At the heart of our being as persons is the demand that we and all that is best in us, all that we value most, shall survive, shall escape the relentless disintegration of the matter-energy universe. That means that the organizing and unifying tendency of life, as it has been going on in our corner of the universe, shall continue, for if the unifying tendency ceases, or relaxes its forward pressure, the organic and differentiated unions it had built up will surely fall back into fragmentation and death. For our lives to be meaningful, according to Teilhard, they must succeed in continuing the creative work of evolution. The only way to escape destruction is to be built into the next level of organized unity.

In Teilhard's view, all of evolution has progressed by a series of creative unions. More complex and more conscious beings are formed by the union of less complex and less conscious elements with one another. The elements unite with one another in terms of their characteristic energies, because of their affinity for one another. Subatomic particles unite to form atoms, atoms unite to form molecules, molecules unite to form cells, cells unite to form organisms. This same pattern of creating something new, something more complex and more conscious, by the union of the less complex and less conscious, recurs at each of these levels. It is because we can look back and see the pattern, see it recurring, that Teilhard believes we can legitimately extrapolate and project the pattern into the future, looking forward to another creative union in which *we* will be the uniting elements.

However, at this point evolution meets a situation that is unique in its history: the uniting elements in our case are free agents. We will not automatically unite merely because of some natural affinity. Since each of us is free, we can each choose whether we will enter into the proposed union, or not. Thus the union, the new being, the next creative advance of evolution, will come about only if we freely consent to form it. This is why Teilhard says that the whole cosmic enterprise now hangs on our decision: *we are evolution*.

It is a grand option that confronts us, the crucial option not only of our history but of the universe's history—at least this is so if the cosmogenesis does not have a contradiction built into it and if our desire to survive is possible of fulfillment. At this point the universe will either go forward into the creation of higher level unities, or else it will eventually fall back into the dispersed homogeneity of maximal entropy. It all depends on what we choose to do.

Human Energy

Consider what is involved, what we are being asked to do, if we take this option seriously. In order for us to unite with one another to form the next creative union, according to the same pattern that the atoms and molecules and cells followed before us, we must share with one another our characteristic energies. It is the energy-sharing that forms the bond in each case. What is *human* energy? Characteristically human energy? It is not just physical energy or chemical energy or biological energy. It is the energy of thinking, or knowing, and the energy of loving, or willing. It is this most intimate energy of ours that we are asked to commit to the new union. In other words, we are being asked to give ourselves *as persons* in order to create a higher level new being. From the union of persons, in Teilhard's language, will come the *hyperpersonal*.

Now, our personal energy isn't used to such patterns. It customarily runs in quite a different way. We habitually see the world—think of it and know it—in terms of how it is advantageous or disadvantageous for us individually, or for us in whatever group we have identified ourselves with—family, nation, political party, religion, race, gender. Similarly, we will and choose and love whatever advantages us and reject whatever disadvantages us. Our energy currents are egocentric, even if the ego is a group ego. The current flows out from the ego, grasps what is good for the ego, and flows back to the ego.

That energy pattern cannot form a creative union, because it tries to assimilate all other beings to the being of the ego by consuming them, that is, reducing their meaning to what they mean for the ego. It implicitly denies that the others have meaning in and of and for themselves. Creative unions are made by an *equal* uniting of the participating elements, not by the domination of some participants over others. Domination cannot produce anything *new*. It leaves the being and the consciousness of the elements exactly where it found them. Only when all the elements unite with one another with equal value and dignity, equally subject to the metamorphosis worked on them by the new form that they make together, is there a genuine advance in complexity and consciousness.

This analysis applies both in the microphase and in the macrophase. In our present mentality, not only are plants and animals regarded as existing for the sake of human beings, but lower caste people—females, the poor, whatever ethnic types are currently despised by those in power—all these are regarded as existing for, having their meaning in terms of how they relate to, the higher caste people. Race relations, international relations, business relations, as well as one-on-one personal relations, are ordered by these egocentric energy currents. The next creative union cannot come from them.

If we are to make the grand option in favor of forming the new hyperpersonal being, we will have to redirect these energy currents. And it will take energy to change them. We can foresee *that*, even before we make the option. Therefore, it will also take energy even to make the option, to commit ourselves to the intention to change our personal energy currents. We can see what it will mean, how profoundly we will have to change, how much self-love we will have to sacrifice, how our whole pattern of thinking and desiring, seeing and valuing, will have to be radically transformed. We will have to forsake privilege, we will have to respect and value all persons equally, seek the welfare of each one as we would seek our own welfare. Who is willing to do this? Especially when you bring it down from an abstract, idealized, and romanticized fantasy to your own daily life: *your* spouse, *your* working companions—or those who might share the job market with you—*your* next door neighbors, and so on. This is too hard a saying: who can bear to hear it?

We are in a time of crisis, says Teilhard, like a latter-day John the Baptist. We are approaching a critical threshold. "Repent, for the Kingdom of God is at hand!" Learn to think another way, for the time of opportunity is upon us. But who has the strength to do this? How shall we activate human energy to make this grand option?

I believe that what we need first, and most fundamentally, in order to activate human energy are new images for humanity. After all, most human actions arise out of the *images* we have of the world, of our life in the world, of ourselves and our companions. We do not act from ideas and rational conclusions nearly so often as we act out of our images. Similarly, when we make a crucial option, we are always making, at least on some level, an option for a certain image of reality. With new images of humanity we can gain a better understanding of the structure of the cosmogenesis, the nature of the next union, and the urgency of the decision that awaits us.

I am going to propose an image—that of Holy Communion— which at first may seem not new at all. I say that it *is* new because most of us have never really seen ourselves and all our world in terms of it. (Never mind for our present purposes that it is associated with a particular religious tradition: we earthlings are the heirs of all the traditions and may take to ourselves whatever insights and symbols have arisen in whatever context.) I think the Holy Communion can be a good image for us if we understand what is involved in it and if we allow for—as we must with all the truly great energizing images—what is in it that we do not yet understand. But before I can show why I think it is a good image, I have to present a brief preliminary exposition.

The Human "Center"

A new image of humanity that will help activate human energy to make the grand option must enable us to do what the next creative union requires: that we share our characteristic human energies, that we unite, as Teilhard says, "center to center," from what is deepest in ourselves. Furthermore, the nature of the act of uniting has to be considered. So there are two important points: what constitutes our "center" and how the centers draw together, or are united.

I pointed out already that the energy currents that form domination patterns are incapable of activating the next creative union. In Teilhardian terms, it is a question of whether radial energy is being activated or whether only tangential energy is being expressed. By "tangential energy" Teilhard means that energy which relates elements to others of the same degree of complexity, such as atoms with other atoms, or cells with other cells. He says it expresses itself in mechanical effects. People also can relate to one another this way, in terms of superficial qualities of our social roles and positions. It is emphasis on this that leads to stereotyping and to people being reduced to statistics. All totalitarian systems operate this way, and we also, insofar as we hold images of other people and ourselves according to their and our social roles and positions, are buying into that same mentality.

Radial energy, on the other hand, is the energy that draws beings forward to higher levels of unification, complexity, and consciousness.

It involves joining what is most central in ourselves, most interior. It is only when this central selfhood is committed to the union that a new type of being is created. Thus the union is made from the *inside out*, not from the outside in. Each successive creative union—from atom to molecule to cell to organism—produces a being that is more intensely centered, that has more interiority and more self-possession. Therefore, each successive union has had to reach down deeper than the preceding one, in order to unite the deepest interiority, the most central selfhood, of the beings concerned. For people, this means that economic and political and technological unions are not sufficient. We must be joined together precisely as *persons*.

What is it to be a person? What is deepest and most central in our sense of selfhood? Clearly, it is not the sort of thing by which we may be classified and stereotyped. Think of all the categories into which you might be placed by a cosmic census taker, according to your sex, age, race, marital status, economic class, nationality, occupation, astrological sign, temperamental type, personality characteristics, tastes and preferences, and biographical history. The very heart of you must lie deeper still than these tangential relations and must be able to make you be *you*, even if these class characteristics should be different. It lies in the *you* that is able to initiate actions, in the *you* that is a free agent.

This center of freedom in ourselves is usually called the will. It is important to distinguish the will from emotions, desires, and other feelings that come and go with the circumstances of life and to understand and experience the will as unconditioned freedom, always capable of exercising its own act. The reason that this is important is that we are called in the next creative union to unite ourselves with *all* other persons. We can't depend on just naturally liking all other persons: usually we like only certain types, while other types we tend to avoid or to reject, either because we don't find their personalities agreeable, or because we have had unpleasant relations with them in the past, or because we see them as threats to our future well-being in some way.

This is the difficulty that we must overcome if we are to succeed in actually forming the creative union that will be our salvation and constitute our meaningful life. Our emotions and feelings are usually subject to the ups and downs of our circumstances in life and cause us to like or dislike other people. So if we are to effect the creative union with *all* other persons, we will need to do it from a center in ourselves that is free of the fluctuations of these circumstantial feelings. The center of freedom is the will.

When we say that the will is free, we mean that its act is not determined for it by anything else. The disagreeable personality of another does not force the will to reject that individual. A history of having suffered injustice from a certain group does not oblige the will to hate all members of that group. Nor does the will have to wait for a pleasant and attractive quality to show up in another person in order to be moved to accept and to join with that individual. The will doesn't have to remain inactive until the prospect of an advantage to itself moves it. The will is free with *creative freedom:* it can initiate its own movement, even without any stimulus in the environment.

Now, this power of self-action in total freedom is precisely what we can all discover to be the most central selfhood in ourselves, the most deeply intimate reality of our being as persons, that which is purely and truly my "I," no matter what my characteristics are for the census taker. My real "I" is not a bunch of statistics but an existential energy by which I live and act. As my own most intimate energy, it has more warmth and vibrancy than my fluctuating emotions. When I love someone from my will, it is a far more meaningful thing that I do, and carries far more of myself, than when I love from my emotions only. The will is the center of vitality in us as it is the center of reality in us. Thus the positive energies that we project toward one another from our wills are profoundly satisfying to us, in a way that mere emotional reactions can never be.

This answers the question, "what constitutes our center?" and we now approach the question of how the centers draw together, or are united. Obviously, the union of free centers cannot be effected unfreely. The nature of the act of unification itself must be such that it thoroughly respects and enhances the nature of the uniting elements. It is at this point that I can propose the image of Holy Communion to explain the act of union that produces Teilhard's hyperpersonal level of being.

The Image of Holy Communion

According to the tradition of the Last Supper, Jesus is represented as the archetypal Friend, the one who gives his own life to those he loves in order that their lives may be more abundant. He uses a very gripping metaphor for this action. He offers himself to his companions under the guise of food and urges them to eat and to be filled with his life and energy.

He is saying two things by this dramatic action: one, he shows that he means to put himself literally *inside* the other persons and, two, that he wishes to *nourish* them. This is his way of expressing his love for his friends. That love is offered to the very heart of their beings as persons. It is not an approval based on their performance, nor an affection elicited by their agreeable qualities. It is unmerited and unconditional, free and creative.

The effect of accepting this love is a whole new image of oneself, other persons, and the way the world is structured. To be loved so profoundly and so securely, beyond all the circumstances of one's conditions and qualities, satisfies the deepest longings of the human heart and, therefore, releases the energy that had been committed to the tasks of defending and augmenting oneself. The loved person has an experience of *being* the interior and central person who is loved in this unconditional way, instead of being identified with the social positions and roles of circumstantial life.

Realizing oneself this way, one is able to perceive other persons as their interior and central selves instead of their social circumstances or temperamental qualities, and one is able to relate to them on that basis. There is now energy available to do this, because one no longer needs to protect oneself against the other person. In fact, there is a surplus of personal energy that can be offered to other persons for their benefit.

At the Last Supper, Jesus follows his own powerful action of giving himself to his friends by enjoining those who accepted him—that is to say, those who realized that he did truly love them that much and in that way—to do the same thing now to one another. They are to love one another as he has loved them. They are to give themselves to one another as nourishing food, entering into one another to increase and enhance life.

There are no limitations on this self-giving. It is not just to those one likes that one makes this offering. People have done good to those who favored them, or from whom they hoped to gain favors, from the beginning of social relations. There is nothing new in that. This is a new commandment, Jesus says, and what is new about it is that it involves a love that issues from the very *center* of the person's being, directed to the *center* of the other person's being, a love that gives *all* that the person is in order to foster the other person's life, a love that is offered to *everyone*, without exception and without condition. The love is not offered to people because they are one's friends; people become "friends" because one loves them.

When this is done, and to the extent that it is done, a new kind of being, a new kind of world, begins to form. Those who love one another in this way, dwell in one another. There is an image of community as mutual interiority: there are no "outsiders." One has the image "I am in you and you are in me." The world of interdwelling persons begins to acquire the features of a living body, as it were, composed of all those who have entered into this union. Perhaps better than calling it a body, we should get even closer to the sense of vitality in it and call it a great *person*, since it is made up of persons acting precisely *as* persons. Can it not answer to what Teilhard called the "hyperpersonal"?

I said that the nature of the act of unification that forms the hyperpersonal must itself be such that it thoroughly respects and enhances the nature of the uniting elements. The Holy Communion does that. Notice that it is energized and united only by the utterly free acts of the persons who make it up. It is impossible for anyone to belong to it unfreely. It is the act of freely loving the others that *constitutes* membership in the communion. Thus becoming an element in this new being activates *most strongly* the characteristic central energy and selfhood of the participants.

Furthermore, these experiences of being loved and loving in turn reveal to us that to be a *person* is to be a self-giving, universally loving, energy-center. The more one actualizes this love, the more one is truly being oneself. In fact, if we do *not* give ourselves to one another in this freely willed love, we will not actualize our deepest being as persons. Thus we can verify the saying that anyone who tries to retain one's life and welfare for oneself alone, will lose one's real selfhood, whereas anyone who gives oneself to one's neighbor will find that one is experiencing a limitless life.

Now I can say a few words about why I think that the Holy Communion is a new and good image of humanity. Teilhard says that this is a personalizing universe: the concept of ourselves as persons has been gradually growing in us culturally over the centuries, just as the reality of us as persons has gradually evolved over the millennia. This image of ourselves—as individuals and as community—that the Holy Communion presents, makes full use of the realization of ourselves as persons. This is the sense in which it is new. It enables us to see ourselves as the reality that is back of all the stereotypes, the classes and categories by which people have thought of themselves for thousands of years. It lets us get to the heart of ourselves, the root of our being, where all persons are of equal dignity and value.

The image of ourselves in the Holy Communion invites us to experience ourselves and one another in terms of our central selfhood, where the energy of personal being originally springs up. And here we can see how the energy currents that I spoke of earlier shift their pattern. Energy flows out from us in the activities of life. If we are selfish and egotistical, or if we simply think of ourselves as isolated beings who need to protect our reality against the encroaching reality of other beings, then our energy currents will move out from us to grasp goods for ourselves or to repulse the aggressions of others and will return to us, making a closed, encapsulating circle. This closed circle of our energy current will shut us up in ourselves and will restrict and cramp us, limiting our being and possibility for growth.

If, on the contrary, we image ourselves according to the Holy Communion, we will let our energy flow out from us to benefit all others—who thereby become our friends—and we will join their lives. This gives us an ever widening life, extending our sense of self-being indefinitely, as we share in the lives of more and more people.

In this way, also, the image of Holy Communion enables us to see both ourselves as individual persons and ourselves as members of the community at the same time. Individual and community are not in conflict but are benefited by precisely the same attitudes and actions. It is our love for our fellows that fulfills us as persons and that simultaneously creates and benefits the community. The microphase and the macrophase are both represented in this image of humanity.

Here, too, we can see that the only way to change the way we behave in the macrophase is to change our way of imaging ourselves in the microphase. This realization of ourselves as persons, independent of the classes to which we belong, is absolutely essential to the salvation of our social life. As Teilhard has so well said, the exhortation to "love one another" represents neither a weakness nor some kind of fad, nor even a psychological luxury; it is essentially a *formal condition for* the achievement of life's organic and technical progress.

Activating Human Energy

That is why love is necessary. But what actually *activates* the love? What concretely and practically liberates that energy? In Teilhard's scheme, this is the role of Omega. Omega is hypothesized as a real person, supremely loving and lovable, actually present here and now, and transcendent of the evolutionary sequence so as to be secure from any possibility of being eventually destroyed by the universe's movement toward increasing entropy. Thus its love can never fail. It must be that which awakens and liberates these energies in us, and it does this by loving us.

The real secret of how to activate human energy to make the grand option of giving ourselves to others is this: Human energy in any person is activated when that person is personally loved by another person. The reason we do not have more of our human energy available for loving each other is that it is mostly tied up in protecting and defending ourselves and in our efforts to "get ahead" or augment ourselves. And the reason we are obliged to devote so much energy to efforts to defend and augment ourselves is that we do not *experience* ourselves—do not have *images* of ourselves—as adequately valuable, securely worthy and acceptable in our own beings. We identify ourselves in terms of the classes to which we belong and the qualities we possess or lack, and we find ourselves inadequate or inferior, rejected or insecure.

We react to compensate for this inadequacy and insecurity by treating other people in ways that in turn reinforce *their* feelings of being inadequate, inferior, and insecure. And they again react to compensate themselves by passing on the evil to those in contact with them.

To break this chain reaction, what is needed is someone who can enable other persons to realize and experience themselves as utterly worthy, valuable, adequate, and secure. This is what personal love does.

Once one person loves one other person in this way and the one loved accepts and is convinced of the love, and thereby experiences security and liberation, the chain of inadequacy-compensation is broken and another type of chain reaction is started. The one loved experiences a great release of tension, a huge relaxation of all the barriers built up for protection, and a letting go of the aggressive operations used for augmentation. All this becomes unnecessary, and the energy that had been bound up in these defensive and offensive devices is liberated in joy and happiness. This joyous energy immediately goes out in love to other persons. It wants to give itself to other persons. It makes the option to be united to them. We have just the opposite of the compensation chain. The one liberated by love now loves others, and each of them, being liberated, loves still others, and the love and liberation spread.

But how to get it started? Someone who *is* free, who already *has* the experience of worthiness and so doesn't have energy restricted to self-protection and self-augmentation, but has abundant energy to give away, such a person must start the chain of love.

This is the role of Omega. This is why Omega has to be a person, not just the name of a community, not a distant ideal, and not an abstraction. Omega has to be a really present person who really loves us, or the operation won't work.

Teilhard is famous for having united science and religion. This is the point at which he unites them. The scientific argument, beginning with the general pattern of nature to make creative unions, has worked its way up to this point at which a supremely loving

Omega-person is required in order to liberate our energy to go further. Then Teilhard turns to his religion and presents the Omega-person in real fact, as he believes, by pointing out Jesus as a person who fulfills the Omega requirements.

Now, in our image of humanity as a Holy Communion, Jesus also figures as the person who does actually love individual persons in this energy-activating way and who starts the chain reaction of persons loving one another. Because of his humanity, Jesus is familiar and tangible to us. Because of his escape from death, he is secure; his love can never fail, and he is able, across time, to be actually—not just imaginatively—present to us now. Because of his abundant free energy, he can liberate love in all who are willing to be loved by him.

It is important to observe that this is always a person-to-person matter. There is here no generalized "love of humankind." Each person loves particular individual other persons. You can love "everyone" in the sense that you are prepared, as *any* one is presented to you, to love *that* one, but it is that particular one in that one's uniqueness that you love. That is how the Holy Communion image for world regeneration differs from all the totalitarian schemes.

All these person-to-person loves cross over one another, like drawing all the diagonals in a polygon of a million sides, so that each person is either actually or implicitly living in each other person. This draws the community together. This is why "Holy Communion" has a double significance. It means the gift of love from one person to one other person; it also indicates the drawing of the whole community by this means into a single, organic, shared life.

For this reason, every individual is called upon to participate in this great act of creating the next stage of evolution, the emergence of the hyperpersonal. No one is dispensable. Each one is of absolute and incalculable value. All our energies must interact in order for the new being to be what it ought to be.

Let us notice with particular care that the personal energies do not *merge* or become *submerged* in some amorphous whole. We do not acquire a kind of oceanic sense of being swallowed up in a great All. Quite the contrary: subjectively, it feels rather like an *intensification* of individuality and self-consciousness, or self-realization. But that individual self-energy realizes itself as a will to the welfare of each other individuality, that the other may be the individual personhood that *it* is called to be. Each person is unique, and it is this uniqueness that is cultivated and celebrated.

Thus the union is not even a matter of "interdependence," as we are usually fond of saying. It is rather a matter of "inter-independence." We are not relating to one another in the Holy Communion in terms of our complementary dependences, or lacks, but in terms of our abundance, our maturity, and our overflowing energy.

And we *have* this overflowing energy. It is the center of our self-hood. The lacks—which are also real and which we can supply in one another—exist on the levels on which we can be classified: as rich or poor, healthy or ill, ignorant or knowing, and so on. Here, too, liberated from the need to invest our major energies in self-defense, those who have goods can freely share them with those who do not. But the central selfhood, the heart, where freedom and the power to love without restriction originally spring up, this is not characterized by lack. We all *have* this, at least in seed form, though we may not have realized it, or activated it, or released it. The experiential *discovery* of it is an essential part of our evolutionary progress at this critical point. There is far more personal energy available to us than we have so far dared to believe.

We need to choose to go forward with our evolution, if we are to make sense of our lives. We need to awaken our energy to make this choice and to form the new hyperpersonal being. This energy sleeps in our souls and only waits to be awakened. We can do four things, singly and together, to awaken and activate it: One, we can understand how the evolutionary development of the universe has been working and can be expected to continue; this prepares us to let go of ways of living that do not contribute to continuing growth and to turn our attention in the direction in which the next creative union can be expected. Two, we can open ourselves to being loved as *persons*, not for any class we belong to or any quality we possess, not for any assignable reason, and we can be willing to accept and believe in the love when it is offered us. Three, to the extent that we have received love, we can love others, freely projecting energies of good will toward each person we touch, seeing ourselves and them in terms of an image such as that of the Holy Communion, in which we each find our personal fulfillment by our creative activities in the complex union of the community. Four, we can take thought and take care that our behavior and our decisions for action in our workaday world embody the sentiments we are learning to experience in these loving attitudes.

If we activate our human energy in this way, we will be able to make the grand option to give ourselves to one another in the next creative union. And when we do this, we will have, in Teilhard's view, experiential assurance that our lives are profoundly meaningful. The human caravan is going somewhere, the human phenomenon is not a cosmic coincidence, but a cosmic climax. All the automatisms of nature, maturing slowly through the eons, are brought to fruition and are transfigured in our consciousness and our freedom, as we take possession of the dynamism of evolution *from the inside* and enable the universe to realize itself as a supremely personal being. The secret of this universe, Teilhard believes, is that it is the embryonic development of the hyperpersonal being centered on Omega. When we, by our free option, will have brought that being to birth, we will know, without any doubt, that we have fully found our meaning.

TWO

Neo-Feminism and the Next Revolution in Consciousness

The excitement of millennial transition, however we date the shift, has emphasized for us two features of our consciousness of which we were already aware: our intense involvement with the sense of the future and our positive feelings toward the notion of revolution. We feel that we are living at the end of an era, on the threshold of a new age, and that what makes the coming age so truly new is that it will be ushered in by some genuinely *radical* rearrangement in our life experience.

When we speak of "revolution," we do not mean something like a mere coup d'état whereby one set of rulers is replaced by another set while the structure of ruling itself remains basically the same—that is only a rebellion. A genuine revolution must be a gestalt shift in the whole way of seeing our relations to one another so that our behavior patterns are reformed from the inside out. Any revolution worthy of the name must be primarily a revolution in consciousness.

There is another twist to our notion of revolution. In our meditations on the future and on our own growth into that future, we have realized that we are evolutionary beings and that what is actively evolving at present is our very consciousness, including our consciousness of ourselves and our consciousness of ourselves as evolving. We may say that we are self-conscious evolution. Looking back over our history, we see that it can be viewed as a series of fluctuations between periods of expansion and periods of consolidation, eras of creativity and eras of conformity, peaceful times and warlike times, ages of small separate states and ages of great unifying empires. Viewed in two dimensions, these fluctuations may appear to be swings of a pendulum, often from one extreme to another. Seen in three dimensions, in terms of the evolution of consciousness, the growth cycle reveals itself to be a spiral, for each time a similar organization of conscious energy comes again, it seems to be on a somewhat higher level that has built on the preceding developments. The revolution that we are currently expecting, therefore, will be also a "revolution" in the sense of being a new "turn" in this mounting spiral of fluctuating but evolving consciousness.

Because the coming revolution in consciousness is truly new, a genuinely radical shift in our basic perceptions, we cannot possibly know just what form it will take. But because it will be another turn on the evolutionary spiral, we may project that it will bear some basic resemblance to its counterparts on earlier levels, as well as distinguish itself by a striking difference from the most recent period. Nevertheless, it will assume and incorporate all preceding stages, preserving and utilizing their advantageous qualities.

There are many ways of approaching a speculation about the new consciousness, but one of the places in which the veil that hides the future from our eyes has worn thin and become partially transparent is the area of the rising feminine consciousness of the world. Indeed, perhaps of all the shadows that the coming age is casting before itself, this is the most revealing, for it touches all levels of our life from the materially biological and technological, through the economic and political, to the emotional and social, the artistic, the religious, and the metaphysical.

Feminine and Masculine Consciousness

What do we mean by *feminine consciousness*? *Feminine* is a polar word, significant by its contrast with its complement, *masculine*. The axis of polarity can be variously chosen, and its orientation makes a critical difference in how we conceive ourselves and our world. The more popular orientations have been along the lines weak/strong, passive/active, soft/hard, submissive/dominant, dark/light, feeling/thinking, domestic/worldly. As a polarity generalized beyond the relations of female and male, these axes have characterized much of the perception, organization, and operation of our world. We have only to think of racial discrimination, economic exploitation, and political domination to realize how the sexual paradigm has modeled many aspects of our lives.

When those who feel themselves oppressed by these social patterns begin to resist, they frequently attempt merely to move from one end of the axis to the other: those who are dominated wish to become dominant themselves. It is important to recognize that such a movement constitutes only a rebellion, not a revolution. It does not herald a new age. A significant future will not be born until the orientation of the axis itself has been shifted.

We need a new perspective in which to view our elementary personal, social, and economic relations, and we need new images in which to represent them mythically to our imaginations, which in turn will direct so much of our life. If the sexual polarity is paradigmatic for larger social relationships, we will do well to explore alternative ways of experiencing it.

First we should note very clearly that the most important thing we have learned recently about the sexual polarity and all its analogues is that it exists within each individual person. It is a complemental structure characterizing every man and every woman. No one is a monopole of this cosmic interaction. Males and females play out symbolically the two aspects of being and consciousness that actually compose all of us. Because the biological relations are relatively simpler and less ambiguous, they can help us to select an axis that will be useful in arranging the rest of our experience.

Three of these relations seem useful at present. First, biologically we are all basically female. Maleness is a genetic and hormonal specialization of the general femaleness. Second, in generation, the paternal act is the quick and simple one of separation and externalization of the generative cell, while the maternal contribution includes being both the locus of union of the two gametes and the long-term holding and nurturing environment of the growing life. Third, the male experience of sexual arousal and satisfaction is comparatively rapid, local, and disconnected from other aspects of life, while the female experience tends to be slow and integral, involving the whole body and the whole life. These contrasts suggest an axis delineating a polarity between the specialized and the general, the analytic and the synthetic, the focused and the wholistic.

Here we can notice that this way of orienting the axis does not represent either pole as more valuable than the other. Obviously, both members of each pair are equally vital to our conscious life, and if we trace the pairing to its ultimate metaphysical origin, the many and the one, we can also say that both members are essential to our very being. We all have masculine consciousness, which is focused, analytical, and specialized, and we all have feminine consciousness, which is general, synthetic, and wholistic. Neither is stronger than the other, or more passive than the other, brighter or darker than the other. There is a complementarity, a life-producing difference, but if its axis is perceived to lie in this suggested orientation, rather than in the popular ones referred to above, then we should derive a genuinely revolutionary vision of our other relations in the world.

The next civilization, in which feminine consciousness, it seems, will be formative, will have its most general characteristics in common with that era of human life that probably preceded the intensely developed masculine era that began at least 5000 years ago. We may call that ancient time the *paleo-feminine age*. It was probably a time of strong group consciousness, a common tribal mind prior to the appearance of the tight circle of ego-consciousness, the awareness of one's individual, separate, isolated self. The unity of the tribe was the ground of all experience. Nature was animated, full of dark forces and mysterious events, and the tribe's life was an integral part of that natural scene. Fertility and the life mysteries, of which women were the obvious symbols, were of central concern. Feelings, emotional patterns, psychic sensitivity, and magic may have occupied a large space in the communal life, especially as compared to the operation of reason and that dispassionate objectivity that we now value so highly.

At least this is how, in the absence of plentiful and unambiguous information, we often imagine the age before the masculine era and how we often characterize the feminine side of reality. This is why it was important to clarify the most general orientation of the feminine/masculine polarity, and why it is important to distinguish the coming age by calling it an era of *neo-feminism*. The paleo-feminine age, as described here, would have expressed a consciousness that was concrete, integral, and unitive, qualities that we expect to reappear in the neo-feminine civilization. But the neo-feminine age will not be a return to emphasis on feelings, emotions, bodily experience, magic and mysteries, or to a fascination with the dark side of consciousness, despite the renewed vogue that some of these experiences are presently enjoying. The themes of unity and immediacy return, but it is not a simple reversal of the pendulum's swing; rather, it is a turn in the spiral of evolution: unity on a completely new level, nurturing the uniqueness of individuals, and immediacy gained by intellectual intuition of whole concrete beings.

We need to stress that neo-feminism, while it is sharply distinguished from "masculism," is not a rejection of the masculine, although we are experiencing a tendency to highlight some of the negative aspects of that consciousness at present.

We may suppose that the masculine era was a rejection of the preceding paleo-feminine age, of its outlook and its values, and we may even suppose that it *needed* to be so, because it is part of the very method of masculine consciousness to work by excluding certain items in order to focus on chosen ones. In the past, confrontation with the huge human environment and the pressure arising not only from the will to survive but from the will to grow, which is characteristic of the human being, made the excluding and focusing consciousness advisable. The range of human senses and human actions, to say nothing of human emotions and human thoughts, is so much greater than that of most animals (very few of whom can perceive or do anything not related to their survival) that the human "world" became gigantic. No one person could work effectively in all of it. The separation of a large subject matter into component parts according to some useful pattern (analysis) and limitation of one's energy, psychic and physical, to some specific area, would seem to have been the only sensible solution.

The *focusing* of consciousness inevitably led to an appreciation of the psychological attitudes necessary to maintain the focus: reinforcement for skill in one's specialty, belief that one's work was a good thing, deserving of honor (or at least that it was the right thing for oneself), camaraderie with others pursuing the same work, refusal to devote one's time or emotional energy to other tasks (which other tasks were therefore scorned or seen as not right for oneself), and so on. This in turn led to the elevation of what we consider the typically masculine virtues: loyalty to one's group; intention to organize affairs—and the whole society if possible—to one's own advantage, that is, to dominate other groups, either overtly or subtly; the ability to make ruthless decisions, and the power to implement them.

The age of masculism produced the world we now live in. At this point, when the qualities of this age have been developed to an extreme pitch and we are beginning to sense a shift to another modality, we may be tempted to concentrate on what we view as its negative aspects: the aggressiveness, the social stratification, the dangerous power we possess over the physical, chemical, and biological agencies of the world. But we should take great care to remember and to realize that it was only by cultivating these very processes and the psychic dispositions that supported them that we were enabled to come to this, the next threshold, where we see that we can transcend these qualities.

The very fact that we are sensitive to social division as injustice, see warfare as horrible rather than as honorable and glorious, and long for cooperation and friendship among all nations is the result of the progress in knowledge and technology achieved by the analyzing and focusing masculine consciousness.

The method of feminine consciousness, however, is different. It works not by excluding but by incorporating. And so the new feminine consciousness of the future can be expected to take up the masculine rational contributions into itself, to hold and absorb them, embed them in the matrix of its own intellectual insights, and eventually to bring forth a new being, a new world.

The wholistic outlook characteristic of feminine consciousness has two aspects, both of which must be stressed and kept in balance: a fundamental and ultimate sense of the unity of the entire human race—even of all of nature—and at the same time an attentive and appreciative sense of the specialness, the unique preciousness, of each particular individual composing that whole. It is precisely this synthesis of the individuals, each retaining its respective value, that constitutes wholeness. The component individuals are themselves concrete wholes. They are not to be identified merely as "parts" of the new whole. Therefore the wholeness of the higher level synthesis arises not from an externally imposed pattern of uniformity but from an immanent principle, working from within the constituent individuals themselves. The new wholeness is thus an achieved unity, not a given unity, and it is essential to it that it be freely achieved. Neo-feminist wholeness is not monolithic or tyrannical: it is organic and differentiating, a processive pattern of freely intercommunicating energies.

The Error of Misplaced Abstractness

In order to see more clearly how this higher level wholeness composed of intercommunicating individual wholes can be conceived, it will be useful to analyze somewhat more carefully the consciousness that produced and sustains our present sense of the abstract individual and the abstract social class. We can then see how the (almost inevitable) exaggeration of this modality of consciousness led to many of the disvalues that we currently recognize and, finally, how the task of the neo-feminist revolution is to correct this exaggeration and to shift our primary perception of persons so as to break the line of development leading to injustice.

The analyzing consciousness began as a great advantage over the vague global co-consciousness that we suspect characterized the early years of human development. The identification of the items of experience by classification—the abstraction of the interesting quality from all the other aspects of the item and the categorization of items according to these chosen qualities—is an intellectual tool of the first order of importance. However, it operates by the power of negation, and this power can very easily run beyond its area of strict usefulness. Let us trace a possible development.

First of all, the consciousness has to be able to screen out, or exclude, all the qualities of a given item of experience except the one quality that is of interest. If *sharp* items are of interest, for instance, then color, odor, place of origin, and many other aspects must be disregarded. This is the first negation. All the *sharp* items must then be seen as belonging to one class and as being distinguished from other items which are *not sharp*. This is the second negation. *Sharpness* is not color and *sharp* objects are not dull, or *unsharp*, objects.

When sharpness is of interest, unsharp objects are rejected and not used. This is the third negation. When sharpness is of interest, more sharp objects are prized above less sharp ones. The behavior of rejection acquires an emotional companion, approval of the sharp object, scorn for the dull one. This is the fourth negation.

The person who is associated with the sharpest objects—the one who finds them, produces them, or possesses them—is associated with the high regard accorded the sharp objects, while the person who has the opposite association receives also the scorn due his implement. This is the fifth negation.

Finally, just as all the sharp objects were perceived as forming one class, so all the persons possessing sharp objects come to be seen as forming a single class, and the emotions of honor or scorn now attach to the classes as such and can be extended to persons associated with their members who would otherwise not themselves be members of the classes. Depending, of course, on how important the original quality was—and the sharpness of tools and weapons might be a quite important quality—the honored class may succeed in generalizing not only its membership but also its privileged position, so that it is honored not just for its sharp implements but in general, as a social class. It will then expect privileges that have nothing to do with sharp implements and will tend to dominate other members of the society in every respect. The analyzing, evaluating, and generalizing consciousness can thus develop in this gradual and apparently quite natural way, and the resulting domination paradigm will be seen as the normal way to relate members of society to one another.

The social classes established by this method of negation can be quite stable. The abstraction of some one quality makes the identity of the class and of its members clear and definite. A sense of self-identity for the class and for each member becomes possible in terms of this ordering principle. Because the identification is so simple, so clear, and so definite, it can bring a sense of security. There is no alternative, no question, no doubt. One has one's place; one knows where one belongs. Even members of the inferior classes will support the system by believing in it and identifying themselves in terms of it. The feelings of the classes toward one another will cover a spectrum of emotions ranging from reverence, deference, respect, and fear to hostility, tolerance, and condescension. These emotions, together with the simplistic ideas formed by the abstraction of qualities, will hold the identification system in place.

Competition for positions of honor within the system does not disturb the system as such. On the contrary, it reinforces it. The attitude that "winning is the only thing" is a powerful affirmation of the method by which the society is structured through abstraction and negation. As Marshall McLuhan realized, "Competition creates resemblance." In order for competition to take place, all qualities but one must be held constant. The competitors are regarded as being alike in every way except the one way that is allowed to vary, and even this quality varies quantitatively. The winner has more of something. While attention is being directed to this limited variation, all the other qualities of the situation are stabilized and homogenized. Especially, the method itself of organizing society is being reinforced: simple abstract sameness, simple abstract otherness, and simple abstract superiority and dominance of some over others.

The error, of course, is misplaced abstractness. When the evaluation procedures that are appropriate within the realm of abstractions are applied to real concrete beings, then the error occurs. John's running may be faster than Joe's, or John's bank balance may be higher than Joe's, but these comparisons among abstractions do not justify the conclusion that John as a whole concrete person is more worthy than

Joe. Identification systems—of ourselves or of others—based on the comparison of abstract qualities are thus based on error: intellectual error and moral error. When we see ourselves and one another in these terms and when we experience for one another the differential emotions of fearful respect or tolerant condescension, we are not seeing the concrete world of real persons but only an emaciated and distorted abstraction of it, and our emotion is as unreal and therefore as wrong as our perception.

This is at least one possible genealogy of injustice. Abstraction, in itself a legitimate and valuable modality of consciousness, is applied to real persons, who are then erroneously valued *as* persons in terms of their rating on the abstraction scale. The *perception* of persons in terms of this dominance ranking gives rise to the *emotions* associated with the domination paradigm and then *behavior* follows the emotions, and we have the multitudinous forms of injustice with which we are only too familiar.

This is why it is not sufficient for us to inveigh against injustice, or to urge that we have respect for all people, or to preach that we love our neighbors as ourselves. As long as we persist in this basic *perception* of people as alienated from one another, valued and judged in terms of various abstract qualities, ranked according to who dominates whom, so long will it be psychologically impossible for us to desist from the practice of injustice. What has to change is the primary perception of being itself. We have to break the identification system based on abstractions and liberate ourselves to perceive persons in their concrete wholeness. This is the meaning of the neo-feminist revolution in consciousness.

Participatory Consciousness

The neo-feminist revolution may actually have been announced some time ago by a unique revolutionary figure of the ancient world, but the announcement must not have been thoroughly recognized, for the error of misplaced abstractness continues to support the domination paradigm in most of our social relations. We are still identifying and locating ourselves and others according to who is dominant and who is submissive, who decides and who obeys, who is to be deferred to and who may be ridiculed. The primary social relation, the sexual relation, is the model for our further relations in economic, political, military, and religious affairs. We tend to think now that the way to break this paradigm is by revolt from the submissive side of the relation. This is why the refusal of the female, the emblem of all submission, to accept this identification and to play this role, presages a profound shift in *all* our social relations and in all our perceptions of the way being is ordered.

But revolt alone will not accomplish the desired transformation—the abstraction/domination perception of being must be displaced by another vision. An alternative vision may already have been offered, one that was introduced, not so much by the revolt of the erstwhile submissive ones as by the resignation of the dominant one. In the New Testament, Jesus is reported to have pointed out to his followers the contrast between the customary way of the world and a new way that he wished to inspire in them:

> You know that the rulers of the gentiles dominate them, and their great men exercise authority over them. It shall not be so among you; but whoever would be great among you must be your servant, and whoever would be first among you must be your slave; even as the son of man came not to be served but to serve, and to give his life as a ransom for many. (Matt. 20:25–28)

Jesus himself set the example when, the night before he died, he washed his disciples' feet and told them: "If I, your 'Lord and Master,' have washed your feet, you also ought to wash one another's feet." But what is he actually doing here? The disciples had been seeing him and themselves in terms of the domination model—recognizing him as the *Dominus*, the Lord, and themselves as his servants—and Peter especially shrank from this inversion of right order, that his Lord should condescend to wash his feet! But condescension wasn't Jesus' point any more than domination had been. Jesus completely reinterprets his action by telling Peter, "Unless I wash you, you cannot participate in me." What he is doing is demolishing the whole pattern of domination and submission. When the characteristic action of a lord becomes the adoption of the role of a servant, then *both* categories perish and a new order is instituted.

This is precisely what happens. "Participation" is introduced as the new paradigm and is vividly dramatized in the supper that follows, for Jesus there reidentifies them all, himself included, as sharing one body and one life. He gives them also another image for this perception of their mutual selfhood: the one vine composed of many branches. And in the discourse recounted in the Gospel according to John, he endeavors to express this new set of relations by saying that his friends—he refuses any longer to call them servants—are "in" him and he is "in" them.

This *participatory consciousness* is what I think is essential to the neo-feminist revolution, and I will try to indicate some of its characteristics.

The first one has already been suggested by contrast with the identification scheme that erroneously values persons as if they were abstractions. Neo-feminine consciousness is a consciousness of whole, concrete, real persons, and it values each one equally. This does not neglect the fact that some people are better at this task or that, that they differ according to certain qualities and can be ranked according to these differences. But all these differences and rankings are *with respect to* some particular quality that has been abstracted from the person as a whole. When this abstraction is appropriate, when this quality is actually functioning, then the ranking scheme is also appropriate. In this sense neo-feminism absorbs the masculine modality of focusing and abstracting for specific purposes. However, it does not stop there or attribute to the whole person the rankings derived from specific functions. When it regards persons as persons, and not as functionaries, it endeavors to be "perfect," even as reality itself is "perfect," that is, whole, concrete, even-handed. The rain, as Jesus observed, falls impartially on the just and on the unjust!

The second characteristic is related to this. The masculine, or abstracting, modality of consciousness operates by negation, as we have seen, a legitimate and valuable operation as long as it is not misplaced. It is a powerful, clear, and unambiguous instrument for establishing functional identities. "This" thing can be distinguished from "that" by the declaration that "this" *is not* "that." This is identification by mutual negation, and it is the basis of our usual logic.

However, when the error of misplaced abstractness is committed, the emotional energy relations of mutual negation are activated also, and we have persons identifying themselves by declaring that they *are not* the other. How often we feel that we can establish and justify ourselves only by being or doing something that no one else is or does. How we seek to value ourselves by discovering what "I've got that so-and-so hasn't got!" How much we need to find security by belonging to a "we" group that negates and is negated by a "they" group.

Neo-feminine consciousness, on the other hand, establishes identities not by mutual negation but by mutual affirmation. The interest is not on how I can promote myself over another but on how I can promote the other in full growth. I affirm the admirable qualities of the other, I reinforce the other's good points, I contribute to the development of the other's potentials; in turn, I experience affirmations coming into me from all the others. I identify the others as those for whom I send out my affirming energies, and I identify myself as one who is receiving incoming affirmative energies.

Jesus said that he was giving a "new commandment" when he urged his friends to "love one another as I have loved you." The old commandment enjoining love of one's neighbors as oneself may have been the best we could do under the identity system of masculine consciousness. It is a *preservative* love, dictated by enlightened self-interest, doing by others as one wishes to be done by, not injuring others as one would not be injured—altogether, as Immanuel Kant remarked, a kind of preventative version of "an eye for an eye and a tooth for a tooth." But the love that goes with participatory consciousness is an outflow of positive energy intending that life should become more abundant. It is a *creative* love, in which one gives of one's own life to foster life in others.

When I love with participatory consciousness, I see that what the other *is* is some of my life-energy living there, and what I *am* is some of the other's life-energy living here in me. I can no longer divide the world into "we's" and "they's." I have an awareness of one large life circulating through all. In some way, my boundary has become less definite, in the sense of being less hard and sealed off. My selfhood has become radiant, streaming out from me, and is found participating in the other even as it is found in me. But I am not engulfed by an all-absorbing unity in which my uniqueness is dissolved. Creative love is exactly the protection and nurturance of personal freedom and uniqueness. It is precisely because a person as a whole is absolutely unique that one transcends all the categories by which abstractive consciousness would classify human life. The single large life in which I participate is a community of whole unique selves who freely form and constitute this large unifying life by the intercommunication of their creative love energies. So, far from being absorbed or dissolved, I feel that as a member of this community my interior sense of self-possession, or self-being, is more intense and clearer, in the sense of being more luminous and more truly "I."

This brings us to the third quality. Neo-feminine consciousness perceives being existentially rather than essentially. Masculine, abstractive consciousness necessarily perceives beings in terms of their essences and sorts out the attributes and properties so that the beings can be categorized. It looks at them from the outside, as objects. Even when we try to look at ourselves, if we are using masculine consciousness, we see an object and we describe ourselves to ourselves as having such and such attributes and evaluate ourselves within each of the corresponding attribute categories. This gives us a pseudoself, and the pseudoself gives us a lot of problems, as we well know.

Participatory consciousness identifies itself precisely as actually existing, experiences itself in the act of existing that transcends all the essence categories, and it enters sympathetically into the lives of others as existing in a similarly transessential way. This explains the sense of luminous aliveness that characterizes the participatory consciousness, the awareness of being vitally an "I," a self, an indefinable being who is sheer life-energy. Perceiving itself this way, the participatory consciousness perceives other persons this way, too, as if they are radiant life-energy centers, intense senses of being living "I's." It shares in this "I live" consciousness of the other. Its perception is: "because I live, you are living also."

This existential perception is not a gut feeling but an intellectual intuition. Feelings, or quasi-instincts, perceptions on the existential level that were unaccountable, not understood, therefore mysterious and dark, did characterize—we may suppose—the paleo-feminine consciousness, vestiges of which we still carry. Masculine consciousness was a tremendous advance over this, for by its method of abstracting the essences, focusing on them and organizing them, it succeeded in giving accounts of its operations, in being self-consciously reasonable. Consciousness became clear and critical, although limited in its logical conclusions to the abstract classes that are its proper subject matter. This is a powerful method and obviously we intend to retain it and to use it, recognizing its limitations.

The neo-feminine consciousness, however, is still something else, not the paleo-feminine instinct nor the masculine reason, but the next level of advance, an intellectual intuition, or insight. It is an act of the spirit, not of the emotions (although there is spiritual, that is, free or nonnecessitated, affectivity associated with it). It grasps what it understands as a whole, as a real concrete being, as a unique instance or self, not as a member of a class or in terms of its categorizable attributes. It does not argue to what it sees but sees it directly, without mediation, by simple inspection. It does not undertake to prove things to itself, for its vision is self-validation. It is conscious of itself and understands clearly what it is doing and how it is doing it. It is a supreme act of cognition that is simultaneously an act of spiritual sympathy.

It is as though one centered oneself in one's own subjective—that is, active—being and also entered into the subject-beings of others. In fact, when sympathy, or experiencing together, reaches this point, the sense in which the other is "other" has undergone a profound change. When expressed in the language of analytical negation-consciousness—which most of our language necessarily is—this state of affairs appears as a paradox. The apostle Paul declared: "I live, yet not I, but Christ lives in me."

Is it really possible to enter into such a transformed state of consciousness? Yes, it must be possible, for some persons have succeeded in doing it. And yes, probably it is possible even for whole populations. There is a vast future ahead of us, and surely our present state is not our ultimate state. So many apparently unlikely things have already happened in the course of nature's history that it is not unreasonable to suppose that even this might come to pass.

No one claims that it would be easy to undergo this transformation. Even Jesus described it as like being born all over again, or as like dying and coming back to life in a quite different way. As we said in the beginning, only a gestalt shift in our patterns of primary perception—only a change of this degree of profundity—would constitute a genuine revolution.

The real question is, do we want a revolution? And if so, do we want it to go in this direction? These are questions only we can decide. We may argue that the proposed direction seems to fulfill the general pattern of nature in its evolutionary spiral of balance, recapitulation, and growth by recurrence of pattern; or we may argue that some other direction of development is more desirable. Whatever the direction, our development will not come upon us automatically by some secret mechanism of nature itself. Any evolutionary advance made in our consciousness now will be made by the exercise of our own freedom. It is up to us to meditate on the meaning of our selfhood, on the alternative states of consciousness open to us, on the patterns by which we may order our experience, and on the kind of growth we want to have.

We already feel that we are people of the future, people of a great frontier whose borders are unknown. We know that it has not yet appeared what we shall be. What we have not yet thoroughly realized is that we are inescapably creators of that future in the most fundamental sense of determining the basic value patterns of perception that order all our other experiences and thereby compose our human "world." None of us can renounce our freedom or flee our consciousness. Neither can we avoid making ourselves, one another, and our world to be as we and it shall be.

We cannot wait for the world to turn, for the times to change that we may change with them, for the revolution to come and carry us round in its new course. We ourselves *are* the future and we *are* the revolution. If and when the next revolution comes, it will come as *we* turn and the world turns with us.

THREE

From Dominus *to* Amicus

Contemplative Insight
and a New Social Order

> "I no longer call you servants . . . but friends."
> — John 15:15

Many people say that it is difficult to practice contemplation in our "secularized society." But our society is "secularized" precisely because contemplation is not adequately practiced. These two work in a circle: the general environment of our consciousness either supports or hinders our contemplative life, and our contemplative life (or the lack of it) gives (or fails to give) spiritual dimensions to the surrounding world.

I contend that we, as contemplatives, can do something about this. The role of our contemplative insight is, first, to see clearly that this "secularization" derives from a loyalty to what I call the Domination Paradigm—*Dominus*—as the basic method of organizing the world and, then, to see that spiritual dimensions will be realized in the world when the world is experienced instead in terms of *Amicus*, the Friendship Paradigm. When we do that, to the extent that we do it, we will be able to move into a new social order.

This is, of course, an ambitious and radical undertaking. Contemplation itself is an ambitious and radical undertaking. As Jacques Maritain tells us, it is a direct experience of participation in divine life.[1] It is awkward to attempt to speak of it, because one of the principal things that must be said about this participation is that it transcends all concepts. All the words we use to point toward it, therefore, are necessarily inadequate, since they were drawn from experiences of quite a different modality of existence—namely, the world of multiple and finite things.

By agreement we may retain the words "experience" and "consciousness" in their most general senses, so that they may not be discredited by the argument that the contemplative union is not an "experience of" anything or a "consciousness of" anything. I will speak of contemplation as an experience and as a consciousness, meaning that it is an experience and a consciousness that transcends the usual subject/object polarity.

Our usual consciousness is a consciousness articulated by concepts. The contemplative consciousness is inarticulate—or rather we should say that, although it has an absolutely inarticulate aspect, it also has a creative aspect that operates by a principle of articulation quite different from that which we are accustomed to using. Both of these aspects seem important: The first, because it locates the initial difficulty we have in attaining a contemplative consciousness; the second, because it recognizes that the contemplative mode of connection may be uniquely articulate and that we need not suppose the only alternative to our present way of differentiating and relating is unity in the absolute, transcendent emptiness of contemplative silence.

"Secularized" consciousness is structured by concepts, which are symbols for, or representations of, classes of descriptive qualities. We use these concepts to analyze and organize the material world and the metaworlds we construct of the first and second level abstractions drawn from the material world. What happens in this modality of consciousness is that we fix on the objects of consciousness, the concepts, as if consciousness consisted of concepts.[2] I want to call attention to the way of being conscious of the concepts as distinct from the consciousness of the concepts themselves. It is the way of being conscious that must change if contemplative consciousness is to be achieved. It is not a question of merely altering the contents of consciousness, but a much more radical transformation.

The precontemplative way of being conscious is by attention to the contrasts among the concepts of the various descriptive qualities of beings. We notice, identify, relate, and arrange the contents of our consciousness by the contrasts among them; and we value, prefer, and attach significance to them by contrast. But the contemplative consciousness is intensely absorbed by that which has no contrast. If one wished to argue—however fallaciously—that there are contrasts in the divine life, still the contemplative consciousness does not identify the divine life by means of the contrast and is not absorbed in the divine life on account of the contrast. Here interest, value, meaning, intelligibility, devotion, and commitment are all at their absolute peak, unsupported by contrast consciousness.

Good and evil, being and nonbeing, are not polarities in the sense that right and left, concave and convex, or north and south are. The latter pairs are defined and known only by reference to one another, but good and evil are not reciprocals. Evil is defined through reference to good, but good is not defined through reference to evil. A common error of the precontemplative consciousness is to claim that no one could appreciate goodness without experience of evil. This is the claim of contrast consciousness that its method of identifying and valuing is the only possible way of being conscious.

This begins to show why the secularized consciousness is such a hindrance to the contemplative consciousness. The secularized consciousness believes that the world is made up simply of various separate beings, which can be known and valued by their differences, their contrasts with one another. It applies this assumption and this method of being conscious (knowing and valuing) not only to "the world" but to itself and to God. Everything is objectified. Every being has its identity, meaning, and value by reference to other beings with which it is contrasted.

The immediate consequence of this is that every being must maintain itself by maintaining its contrasts with other beings. This means that it must be different in its descriptive qualities and it must be different in its value. To the extent that it is "the same as" or "equal to" others, to that extent it loses identity.

When these principles are applied to the social world of human beings—our most immediate environment and the one most significant for us in our effort to attain contemplative consciousness—it is not hard to see what is bound to happen. We will be constantly on the alert to protect and enhance our descriptive qualities and our rank or status. We will have difficulty knowing "who we are" unless we can identify the classes to which we belong, classes descriptive of our bodies, our temperaments or personalities, our histories, our memberships or allegiances, and our choices.

Because the value contrast is always a matter of preference and honor, there has to be a loser for every winner. This is why this modality of consciousness can be said to be modeled after the "*Dominus* paradigm." It ranks beings according to which dominates. The lord/servant relation is the archetype of these contrasts. Our society does not like to use these exact words any more, but the relationship is still intact. Our organizations (including religious organizations), and even our personal relations, are still set up in terms of power and authority rights and deference behaviors. The rank gained by some particular functional status, such as wealth, office, or skills, usually carries over into a generalized social status for the person as such. Of course, those who lack such status suffer a correspondingly generalized domination by those who possess it, and are obliged to serve them.

It is in the context of this type of "secularized" consciousness that the call to contemplation, to participation in divine life, is issued, together with its creative corollary, "Love your neighbor as yourself." But it is impossible to answer this call as long as the *Dominus* paradigm and its contrast consciousness are in place. As long as oneself, God, and the neighbor are regarded as "other," either dominating me or being dominated by me, we will be strictly unable to attain contemplative consciousness and unable to love our neighbors as ourselves.

The reason is not far to seek. It is a failure to plumb the full force and mystery of this commandment, to excuse it as meaning merely that we ought to love our neighbors *as much as* we love ourselves, or *as if* they were ourselves.

The solution is not to declare that "the neighbor" and "oneself" are "the same," as if the only alternative to distinction by mutual negation were to collapse everything into an indiscriminate unity. The solution will be to find another modality of consciousness in which the method of articulation preserves differentiation without using negation and domination. This is what creative contemplation can do for the secularized world, but only if the contemplative consciousness first frees itself from these very principles of the secularized world.

The contemplative consciousness is frequently intertwined with a religious consciousness, which is almost always built up by metaphors, models, and images of beings as they are differentiated and related by each particular religious tradition. A very common metaphor in religious consciousness is the use of the term "Lord" to describe God. When this is done, the lord/servant paradigm naturally becomes the model for all other relations, political, social, emotional, even metaphysical and logical, as we mentioned in treating of identity by mutual negation. Curiously, but inevitably, this very paradigm militates against the attainment of what these same religious traditions usually hold out as their highest ideal: the realization of the union of the personal soul with God.

We live in this kind of world, and it is inside this consciousness shot through with lord/servant images that we struggle to rise to contemplative consciousness. It is interesting to look around us, at the national world, the military world, the business world, the world of sexual and family relationships, and the religious world, and count the ways in which we are reminded to identify ourselves in terms of our descriptive qualities and their value rankings—in terms of our bodies, our class memberships, our histories, our positions in organizations, and so on. A thousand times a day we are driven away from finding our true being in participation in the divine life and are urged to locate ourselves in our assigned niche in the dominance hierarchy.

Again, the solution is not merely to deny the conclusions drawn from the assumption that "Lord/servant" is an appropriate model by which to be conscious of ourselves and God. Rather what is needed is to find an alternative model that addresses the whole question in a quite different way. I think that this is the proper business of the quest for the contemplative life.

This is the prerequisite to that creative contemplative consciousness that can begin to incarnate the Kingdom of Heaven on earth. Until this is done, we will continue to experiment with contrived unions, which give the outward appearance of harmony and cooperation, but are actually fragile balances of individual self-interests. The "enlightened" self-interest that sees the long-term advantages of cooperation, honesty, and a certain amount of altruism is not a fundamental solution to the problem of relations among people. Complementarity, needing each other, interdependence, "symbiosis," are often praised as the mature, desirable, and fulfilling way for people to relate to one another. But all these are at bottom variations on self-love, erotic movements of our selfhood-energy which, however far-flung their detours and complicated their gyrations, intend to come safely home bearing goods for the self. This is the mark of eros, that it loves the beloved because the beloved is somehow good for the lover. It may gain this good either by dominating the beloved or by surrendering to be dominated (and protected) by the beloved. In spite of all the interlocking of individual needs and desires, this movement leaves the descriptive self essentially where it was: in its isolation and in its contingency and, therefore, in its insecurity and its anxiety.

The contemplative's message to the world is that real union and harmony among people will be had only when this erotic movement of our consciousness-energy is replaced by the agape movement, which goes out from the lover toward the beloved to seek the good of the beloved, and rests in the beloved. By this one movement the lover promotes the being of the beloved, the being of the lover (by exercising the lover's characteristic activity), and the union of the two. The lover is radically relieved of isolation and suffers no insecurity by so acting, because the more love-energy is expended toward the beloved, the more the lover is established as a lover. Clearly, the mutual exchange of such agape-energies would constitute a genuine union, because its very basis is the act of uniting, while the enlightened self-interest cooperatives are pseudounions, because their foundation is the essential isolation of individual self-interest.

The self that can emit agape-energies is not the descriptive self. The descriptive self is obliged, by its very constitution and definition, constantly to seek its own maintenance, its own good, and to defend its own well-being. Therefore, another type or level of selfhood must be discovered that can be the subject of agape.

It is a matter of shifting the sense of identity, the referent of the word "I." Some might say that the contemplative should give up the word altogether. But it is only necessary to give it up if it continues to mean something other than the true self. There always remains a center of consciousness, and it is to this center of consciousness that the word may continue to refer. The question is where this center is located and how its identity is defined.

Thomas Merton makes a distinction between what he calls the true self and the false self. The false self, he says, is "the self that exists only in my own egocentric desires" and that is regarded as "the fundamental reality of life to which everything else in the universe is ordered." The things that are ordered to it include "pleasures, . . . experiences, . . . power, honor, knowledge and love." In a vivid and very accurate image he says:

> I wind experiences around myself and cover myself with pleasures and glory like bandages in order to make myself perceptible to myself and to the world, as if I were an invisible body that could only become visible when something visible covered its surface.[3]

This false self, often called the empirical ego, is what I have called the descriptive self. It is a self that is defined, identified, and located by descriptive qualities and that gains membership in the classes to which it belongs in order to establish its differences from other beings, acquiring such precedence over them as it can. It is the self that is identified by mutual negation and that relates itself to other selves largely in terms of dominating or being dominated.

The task of advancing toward contemplation is the task of transcending this identification and moving toward identification with the true self, which Thomas Merton points to: "At the center of our being is a point of nothingness which is untouched by sin and by illusion, a point of pure truth, a point or spark which belongs entirely to God."[4]

We have to begin to be careful how we use the word "I." If we genuinely experience our selfhood as located in the descriptions and defined by mutual negation, and if it is from this point that we look out on the rest of the world, then we correctly speak of "our" inability to do anything for "ourselves," of "our" passivity with respect to God's action upon "us," and other similar expressions. "I" means for us the separate, empirical ego. Nevertheless, stress on such statements, or discussion of the spiritual life exclusively in such terms and from such a point of view, does not help the would-be contemplative to pass over into the realization of participation in the divine life, because these statements continue to call up the identity-image of the empirical ego, with the suggestion that in all humility we really ought to identify with it and locate ourselves there.

But contemplation is the direct and actual experience of participation in the divine life. Those who do experience it often try to convey their realization by saying such things as, "I am in God and God is in me"; "it makes no sense to distinguish between us, as if I were one being and God some other being"[5]; or, "I am in you and you in me."[6] The "I" who speaks here is the true self and is not to be identified with the descriptive self. From the perspective of the true self, the descriptive self is the winding sheets of Merton's metaphor, and not really a "self" at all, and therefore not spoken of as "I." The true self, "I," looks back on those descriptions and says "they" of them: "They are all destined by their very contingency to be destroyed."[7]

The center of consciousness now locates itself in the sinless point of nothingness that is the true self and looks back on the descriptions as something else. This is why the person who is immersed in contemplative consciousness may use the word "I" in ways that seem to those in precontemplative consciousness to be stupidly inaccurate or arrogant to the point of blasphemy. One has always to remember, as Merton says, "that the *identity* of the *person* which is the subject of this transcendent consciousness is not the ego as isolated and contingent, but the person as 'found' and 'actualized' in union with Christ."[8]

One who sets out deliberately to shift the sense of identity from the empirical ego to the transcendent self usually adopts a double method: modification of behavior and meditation. The two interact.

The behavioral changes begin with the cessation of actions that are harmful to neighbors and of actions that are obviously vain or greedy or otherwise selfish. In their place are put positive actions of generosity, helpfulness, concern for and service to others.

Finer modifications involve something called "self-denial." This seems at first sight to mean denying to oneself something that one wants or perhaps even needs, with the intention of gaining detachment from that good and that desire. The real meaning of "self-denial" is not so much to deny something *to* the empirical ego as it is to deny that one *is* the empirical ego. Meditation focuses the consciousness-energy on the transcendent level. Sometimes this is done ecstatically by focusing on God instead of "oneself," until one awakens to the fact that one is actually living there in the divine life; sometimes it is done enstatically by drawing the consciousness-energies in to the center of the self, away from the superficial layers of the descriptive being, until the divine transcendent being is realized at the innermost point. As Thomas Merton says, "There is only one problem on which all my existence, my peace and my happiness depend: to discover myself in discovering God. If I find Him I will find myself and if I find my true self I will find Him."[9]

Both the asceticism and the meditation help to strip off the accustomed descriptive identity, "I am so-and-so." When all those predicates fall away, one by one, only the "I am" is left, empty and unmodified, not even known to itself by reflection but only by a noetic coincidence with its own existence. Then the transcendent self is revealed as one that says, simultaneously with its unlimited "I am," "May all be and be abundantly." There is no such thing as a transcendent self that is not a luminous source of agape-energy. As soon as the descriptive coverings wound around it, of which Merton spoke, are removed, the radiant character of the true self is evident. Its whole reality is to be a self-giving being. That is the kind of being it is.[10]

In the ecstatic context, one says, "God is agape." But God cannot be seen, cannot be looked at, cannot be objectified; God can only be coincided with, or known from the inside, by experiencing in one's own subjective consciousness the radiant power of outflooding agape that is the divine life. In the enstatic context, one discovers at the center of one's own being an enormous influx and "through-flux" of agape-energy that is clearly transcendent with respect to all the phenomenal layers of one's being and thus "other than" they. In the first case, in finding God, one found oneself, and in the second case, in finding oneself, one found God.

In both cases the self must identify itself by saying to the divine life, "I am in you and you are in me." There is no way in which the transcendent self, or true self, can identify itself by saying, "I am I insofar as I am not-you." This is the moment of contemplative insight into a new paradigm of personal identity. The essence of God is agape and the essence of our true self is participation in this agape. This means that one's identity is expressed by saying, "I am I insofar as I give myself to you, and live in you." The insight is the double one that the true self is transcendent of the descriptive layers of being *and* that the true self is an outpouring of creative love-energies toward all.

This is also where God is revealed and experienced not as *Dominus* but *Amicus*, the Lover, the Friend. The contemplative is the one who consents to this incredible intimacy, and all that it implies, and does not resist it under the guise of piety. We can be like Peter at the Last Supper resisting Jesus' offer to wash his feet and, insisting on calling God "Lord," shrink from cooperating in the act that obliterates the roles of lords and servants. Or, in a grand option, we can agree not to frustrate the divine life in its effort to give itself to us thoroughly and to build up in us an image and incarnation of its own interiority.[11]

The Friend is the one who gives completely, gives one's own life, shares everything, becomes food for others.[12] Agape is a *spondic* energy, poured out as a libation, a gesture of reverence and worship, an endless stream of devotion.[13] Those who identify themselves with this true selfhood, and thus experience participation in the divine life, all radiate agape-energies toward one another. Instead of the empirical ego's identity by mutual negation, we have identity by mutual affirmation. The Friend says to the beloved, "You and I are one; whoever sees me, sees you and whoever sees you, sees me. Whatever any do to you, they do to me; what they do to me, they do to you; what you do, I do; and what I do, you do."[14] The Friends' lives flow together, like sunshine pouring into a room through several windows, as St. Teresa of Avila said. The windows may be different, even separate, but it is all one light in the room. The metaphor of confluence, even *inter*fluence, is helpful, because it shifts attention from a concern with the static boundaries of defined natures to a concern with the dynamic activity of transcendent persons, away from the separateness of the windows and onto the wholeness and the continuity of the light.

Because all parties to the *Amicus* union are radiant beings rather than bounded and defined beings, certain questions that make sense in the world of descriptive beings do not make sense here. For instance, no being can be an object for another. Not only does one subject's "I" not say "it," "she," or "he" *of* another, but the first subject does not even really say "you" *to* another. The relation is perhaps a kind of perfection of the saying of "you," in which one enters so profoundly into the other as to move together with the movement of the other's own subjective consciousness-energies.[15]

One consequence of this is that God cannot be an object for us, nor can we be objects for God. All transitive language becomes inappropriate. In this context, the question of whether the contemplative state is "achieved" by "one's own" efforts, or whether it can only be "given" to "us" by God becomes a nonquestion. Both "God" and "we" are beings whose whole reality is a radiant outpouring of agape-energies. Whatever any of us is to any other is a matter of "giving." "Giving" is our entire life.

All the energetic reality movements that take place in one's subjectivity are in confluence with all others'. Everyone's love is present there, full of the intention that one can be and be abundantly. Each one is full of activity, not passivity. Each one is outpouring energy to all the others.

The confluence metaphor shifts attention from the question of the discrete differentness—or the sameness—of the Friends onto the continuity of the flowing activity of agape itself.[16] It is important to notice that when the assertion of the Friends' being "different" is denied, the assertion of their being "the same" is not affirmed. The question does not make sense in the *Amicus* context, and so does not receive either of those answers.

In general, the modality of being conscious—of discerning form and meaning and assigning value—by means of contrast has disappeared. We need not make comparisons of the descriptions of different beings in order to identify and rank them. There is differentiation, there is articulation, in this union of "amicality." Each participating Friend is identified as the source of an outpouring, or spondic, energy toward all beings. Each one is differentiated by this activity of willing each other to be again an agape-beaming person. They are not differentiated by what they *have* that differs but by the fact that they *are* as they are—that is, by the actuality of each one's act of loving the others. Perhaps we may say that it is an existential differentiation rather than an essential one. Thus it recognizes multiplicity in the same glance in which it beholds union.

Of the two aspects to the contemplative life, one is the breakthrough itself to realization of the participation in divine life; the other is creative action that lives out this realization in the terms of the world. A person who is a "contemplative," therefore, is one who not only enters upon the way that leads toward seeing, or one who preaches and teaches what is seen, but one who puts this vision into practice in every way available.

Especially important for contemplatives is the effort to invent ways to express the contemplative insight. Transition to a new social order is a slow process. It has to be viewed in the context of long-term human evolution, which in turn is a feature of the general cosmic evolution. One's attitude toward it therefore has to be a combination of relentless and courageous forward pressure and imperturbable patience. Finding ways of living that are true to the contemplative insight and also practical and actually workable in the world at its present stage of development is part of the contemplative's vocation.

The first thing that changes in the contemplative's life is one's whole personal outlook. The competitive attitude, the desire to be superior, to be in control, to possess, disappears. At the same time, concern for excellence in personal relations and in all one's works increases, but now this is concern that things be done well for their own sakes and for the sake of other persons. Social ranking ceases to function in a credible way for the contemplative, who treats each person equally with the respect that would be shown, in a ranking mentality, to those of the highest rank.

Functional ranking, where expertise, speed, or efficiency is important—for instance, in service professions, in emergency situations, and in large-scale enterprises—is admitted, because in these cases it is promoting the welfare of the persons concerned, but it is not carried over into a generalized deference behavior pattern in social life at large. Nor does the individual renounce moral responsibility for actions advised or commanded within the chain of functional ranking.

However, the creative contemplative looks for ways to reduce the need for ranking and to replace it by operational structures compatible with "amicality." In particular, there should be a special effort to avoid such ranking structures in religious institutions, which are supposed to have a deep interest in cultivating spirituality among their members. If these institutions can organize themselves without preserving certain positions for privileged classes, and without imposing decisions on those who have no voice in the decision, they will set an example for governmental and economic institutions that will go a long way toward correcting the condition of "secularized society."

The role of contemplative insight here is to insist that the prevalence of domination must not be excused by pleas of divine origin, long tradition, or absence of viable alternatives. It is the contemplative's job to seek out alternatives, to describe and explain them, and to set them up in practice.

Contemplative insight exists in a world mixed with the sense of identity vested in descriptions and positions in dominance ranks. We are going to be "in transition" for a long time and cannot expect to find many unmixed cases. But the new social order manifesting the revelation of personhood as *Amicus* rather than *Dominus* has been growing gradually, and some examples can be indicated, even though they are not perfect and have various other difficulties or even faults. In a time of transition we need to uncover all the new growth we can and foster it in the midst of the old order, helping it gradually to advance.

Among religious institutions, some (usually small groups, such as the Society of Friends) practice decision by consensus and have no power structure at all. Others (e.g., the Episcopal Church in the United States) use election systems modeled after democratic constitutional government. Some religious traditions (e.g., Hindu and Buddhist) may not have "organization" at all but perpetuate themselves by expertise alone, with those who have gained insight training others to put themselves in the position of experiencing it also. In business the trend to involve workers in management and to share with them the company's profits is showing increasing promise. Even a single individual can begin this process, as Madison, Wisconsin landlord Carmen Porce did, when he announced his policy that "tenants should participate in the management decisions," or as Dale Wolf, of the Wolf, Blumberg, and Krotty sales promotion agency in Cincinnati, did when he set up a child care nursery in the firm's offices (with the agreement of all employees) to enable mothers of young children to pursue their careers and remain near their children at the same time.[17] What is needed is insight into the meaning of human life and, then, creative imagination and the courage to carry through an unusual operation. Democracy in general and welfare programs in particular show an intention and an effort to put into practice the contemplative insight regarding the equal, unique, and transcendent value of each person. Of course, we are still struggling and fumbling, but evolution always gropes its way, and the beautiful creations of any age are the survivors of many false starts and failed experiments.

When contemplative insight becomes strong, people do not need challenge and competition to stimulate them to act, to work, and to strive for excellence. They perceive their life as having its value in the act of living, in the process, not in the achievement or in the accumulation of products or in the praise for accomplishment. They experience joy in living from giving to others and so do not need to be motivated by hope of gain.

Another consequence of the growth of contemplative insight for the world will therefore be the increased emphasis on the arts, on things done for the sake of the doing itself, not as means to a further end. We see a good deal of attention in this direction already. This can help to free art from being a business or a matter of "collecting" and playing a market in famous names.[18]

Similarly, contemplative sports can be free to be exercise and fun, not work or business or gambling. Competition is not essential to sport. A sign of rising contemplative consciousness in this area is the appearance of "new games" in which "winning" is no longer an objective.[19]

All this may at first seem like an attempt to "change" human nature. Indeed, the role of the contemplative in society is precisely that.

After all, participation in divine life means doing what the divine life does, and that is creating. Creating is an ongoing activity, expanding from the present into the future, making things that are genuinely *new*. Therefore, the contemplative is not afraid to try to change "human nature" and human institutions.[20]

If we as contemplatives are people who are growing in our realization of participation in divine life, then we are committed to giving up identifying the descriptive self and expanding in the faith and the daring to accept identification with the true, transcendent self who dwells in God and in whom God dwells. When the sense of identity actually makes that shift in perspective, then the contemplative breakthrough or insight is present and full. Because of the nature of the divine life as creative agape, the contemplative life, which is a union with the divine life, must be creative. It is the nature and the vocation of the contemplative to create the world in the image of God, as an interchange of loving creative energies, and as an ongoing process of ever-new improvisations.

Notes

1. Jacques Maritain, *Scholasticism and Politics*, trans. and ed. M. J. Adler (New York: Macmillan, 1940), p. 184.

2. We almost never have any pure percepts; our perceptions are highly modified by our conventional concept systems.

3. Thomas Merton, *New Seeds of Contemplation* (New York: New Directions, 1961), p. 35.

4. Thomas Merton, *Conjectures of a Guilty Bystander* (Garden City, NY: Image, 1968), p. 142.

5. Cf. John 14:9.

6. John 14:20.

7. Thomas Merton, *New Seeds of Contemplation*, p. 35.

8. Thomas Merton, *Zen and the Birds of Appetite* (New York: New Directions, 1968), pp. 74–75.

9. Thomas Merton, *New Seeds of Contemplation*, p. 35 (or p. 36 in later paperback editions).

10. Nevertheless, its act of love is radically free with a "creative freedom" that is deeper than mere "choice freedom." See chapter 4 and chapter 9.

11. See John 17:22–23: "The glory which thou hast given me I have given to them, that they may be one even as we are one, I in them and thou in me, that they may become perfectly one, so that the world may know that thou hast sent me and hast loved them even as thou hast loved me." The suggestion of seeing the Footwashing as the destruction of the lord/servant paradigm and Holy Communion as the institution of the *Amicus* paradigm is developed in the author's "The Holy Thursday Revolution," *Liturgy*, July 1978, and a book of the same title, awaiting publication.

12. Cf. John 13:1; 15:13; 15:15; 6:51.

13. σπονδη, libation; see chapter 4.

14. Cf. John 14:9; Matt. 25:40; John 15:20; Matt. 18:18–20; John 14:12.

15. For a fuller development of the distinctions among the "I-it" relation, the "I-you," and the "I-I," see the author's essay, "Communitarian Nondualism," in B. Bruteau, ed., *The Other Half of My Soul* (Wheaton, Ill.: Quest, 1996).

16. A recent discussion of discreteness and continuity in the context of a new way of thinking of part and whole, as needed in epistemological reflections on quantum mechanics, may be of interest. See Robert Nadeau and Menas Kafatos, *The Non-Local Universe* (Oxford, 1999).

17. For employee-owned businesses, see Jeff Gates, *The Ownership Solution* (Reading, Mass.: Addison-Wesley, 1998). For Porce, see the Associated Press, in the *Cincinnati Enquirer* (September 14, 1980), pp. 1, 6: "The attitudes of the typical investor or landlord give priority to property rights versus human rights," Porce said. "For some, their motives are one-sided, primarily or solely to turn a profit. No wonder there is such distrust of landlords." Porce runs a 280-unit low-income public housing development. Under his management the vacancy rate dropped from 47% to 1%, delinquent rents from 22% to zero, maintenance complaints from 190 to 60 a month, and vandalism is now rare.

For Wolf, see the *Cincinnati Enquirer* (September 15, 1980), p. B1.

18. See Robert H. Frank and Philip J. Cook, *The Winner Take All Society* (New York: The Free Press, 1995).

19. A wide range of business and cultural alternatives are presented in Barbara Marx Hubbard, *Conscious Evolution* (Novato, Calif.: New York Library, 1998).

20. See chapter 8. The question of "changing human nature" is treated in the author's book, *The Holy Thursday Revolution*.

FOUR

Persons in Communion

Perichoresis

In the evolution of our consciousness, we may be said to be standing on the threshold of an era having a renewed sense of unity, of
wholeness, of relations that draw together, of insight that grasps in a
single vision, of universal inclusiveness. We are aware of a desire to
value all persons equally, responding to their integral concrete being
as unique selves, rather than ranking them according to certain abstract qualities by which they can be classified. We recognize that abstraction, analysis, and specialization are useful operations, and we
accept them for their appropriate functions. But we want to experience ourselves as something more than members of a class, bound by
the expectations attached to our social roles. We yearn to join ourselves to all other persons, similarly liberated from class expectations,
experiencing our common humanity and rejoicing in the unity we
have established by sharing our lives in love.

In chapter 2, I have described this consciousness in terms of
"neo-feminism." I have also suggested that it can be seen as the new
paradigm for humanity—and even for the cosmos—introduced by
Jesus in the sacrament of Holy Communion.[1] This last idea, developed further, leads to the conception of our evolved "communion

consciousness" as a *perichoresis,* in the image of the Trinitarian Godhead.[2] The present chapter continues the development from this point, exploring the notion of person as transcendent, outpouring energy that indwells all other persons, so that the energy-exchange unites the many into one and forms a new being.

The Person as Transcendent

If we look probingly at ourselves, at one another, at the relation between us, and ask repeatedly, "Who am I? Who are you? Who are we?," we will gradually discover that there is an important distinction to be made between two levels of our being. These two levels are given different names in various traditions—sometimes the labels are even reversed—but the meaning is usually the same. Suppose we call them "individual (instance of)" and "person."

As long as we answer the "Who" questions with replies such as "I am a housewife," "You are a lawyer," "We are both baseball fans," we have only located the categories by which our phenomena, our appearances, can be classified. We have not really improved our answer much when we respond, "I am a decision maker," "You are good-humored," "We are husband and wife." Even if we exhaustively enumerate all the qualities and functions by which we can be described, we will have indicated only a class, of which the "I" or the "you" and the relationship is an *individual instance.*

If we are to identify ourselves by this type of description and seek to justify our uniqueness in such terms, we will have to pile up more and more predicates, hoping thereby to so limit the class to which we belong that it will contain only one member. But all these abstractions will not catch the true self that we are as a concrete being, and we will probably have the in-depth insight to realize this. We will feel that our "I" is somehow more than all these descriptions and that it would still be itself, even if the description changed.

To realize our self as *person,* we must begin with the concrete being and never leave the concrete being that is our self as actually existing. To know our self as a concrete act of existence, we must give up identifying our self in terms of abstractions. We can usefully identify *objects* abstractly, but if we would know our self, we must remember that it is a *subject* and therefore must be approached by a different method. We cannot *look at* or *talk about* a subject. To do so is to convert it into an object. We must rather *noetically coincide with* our self by experiencing our own existence interiorly.

This can be done by means of a simple exercise. One has only to say "I am such and such," filling in the "such and such" by whatever predicates seem appropriate. Then attend to coinciding with the sense of existing in this way, experience immediately the act of being, identify with the actuality of "I am . . . " all these descriptions. Centering in the sense of actively existing, of being the act "I am," strip away each of the predicates in turn. The concrete subjective experience "I am" will expand as it is less and less bound to this or that particular way of being. With all the predicates removed, the sense of identity will be profoundly centered in the act "I am" alone.

This self is thus transcendent of all the categories in which it can manifest itself. It is not bound by them. It remains capable of manifesting itself otherwise, of presenting itself temporally under different descriptions.

It is this transcendence of the *person* over the *individual* that makes possible the "participatory consciousness" or "communion consciousness" that is our projected next phase in evolution. Each level of evolving consciousness creates a new unity by bonding central energies of the unities of the preceding level. If we ourselves are to become elements for the formation of a higher level being, it is important that we know where to locate our own central energies.

If we try to attain the unity by relations of our outer energies—those associated with the categories and descriptions of our "phenomena"—we will not achieve a true and viable unity of higher order but only a collectivity on this same level where we now exist. The communion we are seeking, and of which we are capable, must take place on a higher—or more central—level of our own several beings. Before we can realize our relation to one another in "communion consciousness," we must learn to identify with our own central, transcendent energy of existence.

The Person as Spondic Energy

When we do center ourselves in the concrete existential experience "I am," we realize that it is intrinsically living and luminous. We no sooner touch this "still point" at the core of our being, this immutable at the heart of mutability, than we discover it as an explosion of energy. Our "I am" is simultaneously a "May you be," also. We find that the energy of existence that we are is necessarily a radiant energy. It streams out from us in every way. It seems to be the nature of that which is "I am" to say "Let it be."[3]

Sometimes it helps to clarify an idea if a strange name is attached to it—it prevents us from bringing up associations we might otherwise have that would confuse the issue. So suppose we call this radiant energy of self-being *spondic energy*, deriving "spondic" from the Greek σπονδή, meaning "libation." It is an outpouring that is an act of reverence, of worship. We experience it as a projection of personal, spiritual, self-existent energy towards and into other persons, and even towards the infrapersonal universe. We will to pour our own life, our own existence, into others that they may be and may be abundantly.

We are revealed to ourselves as energy centers whose energy is naturally spondic, but we also realize that the will to pour ourselves forth is a free act. It is our own act, performed on our own initiative. It is not compelled, not automatic, not unconscious. It is the proper, or characteristic, act of a *person*. To share self-being with another in this central way is precisely what it means to be a person.

The spondic energy does not originate in the outer layers of our manifest being. It is not the act of the individual. It comes from the transcendent center. Nor is it a response to some attractiveness in the outer layers of the other's phenomenal being. It is truly original and spontaneous, arising only from itself. Thus it is always free, always possible.

We may be prevented from "opening up to" an uncongenial personality because our own emotional nature is paralyzed by the mutual rejection experienced on this phenomenal level. But nothing can prevent us from extending to others the life-energy that is the center of our transcendent personal being. It is not hampered by fear, dislike, vanity, vulnerability, or any of a host of similar handicaps that limit the energy relations of our peripheral nature. The central self is full, luminous life, safe from all injury, and is most itself when it is most giving itself.

When we give ourselves to another person, we are pouring energy from our transcendent center into another transcendent center. We know that when we speak directly to another as "you," we are not addressing an instance of a certain collection of qualities, a member of a highly defined class. We are in living contact with another "I am," a subjective existence. How different this real touch is from the experience we have when we think *about* an individual's qualities! The object of our thought is only an abstraction, a carrier of attributes, an item to be identified by classification. The *person* is a unique activity that directs itself towards us with its own energy.

Suppose we have been talking about someone, using third person pronouns and exercising our consciousness on the level where we focus on attributes, relationships, emotions, and judgments—the objective, phenomenal level of categorical reality. Now that person suddenly walks into the room and approaches us. Our whole consciousness changes levels and reorients its focus as we shift from saying "he" or "her" to saying "you." We experience it as a slight shock, a peculiar feeling, a little like guilt, as if some deep sense in us acknowledged that *any* talking "about" a person is a falsification. If we could stop at that moment and carefully attend to the alteration in our state of consciousness, we would realize that a person is an indefinable, transcendent, radiant being who cannot be talked *about* but must be spoken *to*.

When we affirm another with our spondic energy, it is the personal being that is being affirmed, the central selfhood. This should help us to understand how we can practice universal affirmation. Often we find it difficult, even impossible, to project positive energies towards people who have hurt us or who are engaged in behaviors that we consider to be seriously wrong. We feel that we cannot attain "communion consciousness" with those who are separated from us by such barriers. This difficulty arises from a misconception of the level on which the communion is to take place.

To affirm another, we need not sanction his behavior. Indeed, we ought not, if that behavior is evil. And we need not like her, in the sense of feeling an emotional attraction to her empirical personality. Nor need we stand in a pleasant relationship to him based on past experience. All these belong to the "individual," not to the "person." The person transcends the individual's qualities, and the person is spondic energy, fresh every moment, having no past, utterly spontaneous and capable of new manifestations.

Our affirmation, therefore, is directed from our central self, transcendent and spondic, towards the other's central self, transcendent and spondic. Both are beings jetting into the future, unknown from one instant to the next, improvising life as a free creation. Our spondic energy is poured towards the future, for the good of the future. It is not a reaction to the past, but a free promise to the world to come, where all things are still possible.

If our only attitude towards someone is a set of intellectual judgments and emotional feelings based on the qualities he has shown and the behaviors he has produced in the past, then our interaction with him will always be out of date, at least one step behind. We will never be in touch with the person where he really is now, that is, on the verge of the future.

Perhaps these reflections can give us a clue to a deeper meaning of forgiveness. More than a reconciliation between empirical egos, a making-up of estranged personalities, or the more profound joint effort of wrong-doer and wronged to undo the wrong, perhaps forgiveness can be seen as an act of faith in the future and as evidence that one knows where the living being is truly lodged and will not be distracted from it by the dead husks of past deeds. Continuing to pour energy of life and of goodness towards all, we not only do the most powerful thing that can be done to encourage good acts hereafter, but we loosen the hold of false identifications of our self and the other, and we deepen our realization of both of us as transcendent centers of spondic energy capable of communion.

Persons in Communion: Perichoresis

We must not think that transcendent personhood, the fount of spondic energy, is a speculative abstraction and therefore that the act of pouring ourselves into others is an imaginary ideal. In order to follow this exposition, it is essential to remain in the concrete, to experience ourselves as transcendent, as spondic, as forgiving. Those into whom we pour our life are equally concrete, existent persons, not humanity at large. Each person is of such a nature that, if we give up identifying ourselves with the "individual ego" and coincide with ourselves as outflowing energy, we will discover that we can freely and consciously "indwell" every other person and that every other person "indwells" us.

This is not an emotional experience, not a psychic experience, not an altered state of consciousness such as one acquires by drugs or trance or other artificial manipulations of consciousness. It is an evolutionary development of intellectual and moral normal waking awareness. But it does represent a gestalt shift in our metaphysical perception of how we and others are situated in being. Our whole sense of the "location" of our selfhood has to be reordered. This is why this new consciousness is a revolution.

We are accustomed to identifying ourselves in the geometry of existence by material metaphors. "We" are "where" our bodies are. Our reality is limited by our skins. What is inside another bag of skin is "someone else." The space and time of matter-location identifies us and helps us to know *where* and therefore *what* and therefore *who* we are.

Lately, there has been some tendency to turn from the particle metaphor to the field metaphor and to image ourselves as electrifying, magnetizing one another, or as gravitating towards one another, relating to one another's vibrations. This has made our boundaries vaguer but, perhaps, has not clarified the metaphysical relations among us very much. There is the danger that we will begin to take these new energy-field metaphors literally in their turn and identify ourselves with etheric or astral bodies qualified by their vibrations in the same way that the particle bodies were qualified by their spatial location and more static characteristics.

But by practicing noetic coincidence with our inmost transcendent self, and by following it in its outpouring movement, we find that "we" are actually living in the hearts, that is, in the central beings, of other persons. The other persons, moreover, are also fountains of spondic energy, pouring out to all beings, and hence have no fixed location either. We are living in them, but they in turn are living in still others, and so we find that we have no "where" to lay our heads[4] but must be at home in the entire universe, deep in the interior of every being.

The bounded sense of selfhood is utterly dissolved by this discovery. The identity that had been established by energy currents that turned back towards the center when they had come to the edge of their world has lost its foundation and been replaced by an identity that never turns back towards itself but consists of an ever radiant process. One radiant process enters into and unites with another radiant process. "Together" they "beam into" a third and join it. These are only rough metaphors; they are not to be taken too literally or analyzed by an external "thing-identity" logic. The metaphors are indications of interior acts to be made so that one can recover the *experience* that is being described.

The union of one radiant process with another radiant process never comes to an end, for we find that each one we "indwell" is again radiating to all the others, so that the energy goes round in continual circulation, and each participant can truly claim to be "in" each of the others, to be "one" with each of the others and with the whole radiant interaction.

This is the experience on the level of transcendent personal selfhood of the Holy Communion, a "union together" that composes a "whole" in the "sanctity" of mutual self-donation. The Holy Communion in turn can be seen in likeness to that other metaphor of essential being proposed in the Christian tradition, the περικωρησις, *perichoresis*, of the Trinitarian Godhead.

The Trinity is one of the great mythic expressions of the basic mystery of the Many and the One. "Three" being allowed to represent the minimal "Many," the Three Divine Persons are portrayed as so eagerly giving themselves to one another that their acts of life-exchange set up an unceasing circulation of self-energy that constitutes their unity in one being.[5] This being in one another, living and dwelling in one another, where each is not a static being but a living process of further life-donation, is called in Latin *circumincession*. It is a life-movement that goes round and round without beginning, without end. Since each Person becomes most truly the Self that that Person is by performing this characteristic act of giving self-life to the other Persons, the spondic act of self-donation has the unique property of creating simultaneously both unity and differentiation.

Perhaps it is only this act of deliberate self-giving that has this effect. But something that *would* produce such an effect—simultaneously establishing both unity and multiplicity—is precisely what we need metaphysically as the foundation of being and, especially, as the foundation of our being as persons in relation to one another. So if we ask what is the paradigm of Being, what is God, we may answer: God is *perichoresis*, God is the mutual exchange of spondic energy, God is love.

The New Creature

Can the image of the *perichoresis* of the Trinity give us a clue to the nature of our next level of development in evolution? One way of looking at the course of evolution is to notice that each time something on a new level of complexity appears, it constitutes its own unity by the functional exchange of the characteristic energies of the lower level elements of which it is composed. Thus atoms are built up from the subatomic particles, molecules from atoms, crystals, viruses, and cells from molecules, and finally organisms from cells. We may also note that this energy exchange involves a concomitant information exchange. Mutual mingling of meaning and movement is the heart of life, all the way back into the inorganic, which Teilhard de Chardin dared to call "pre-life."[6]

If evolution is proceeding still, and if this pattern yet holds, then it is our turn to serve as "elements" in the formation of the next-level being, a unity born of the exchange amongst us of information and energy, of meaning and movement. It must be the exchange of our *characteristic* energy that constitutes the bonding power of the new creature, not some sharing on a lower level of complexity. This is why it is important for us to realize ourselves as transcendent and spondic and not to expect a truly new way of being to emerge from attempted unions on a biological, emotional, or social level. If we really sense in some deep part of ourselves a desire to unite, not as members of a class, not in terms of our abstract qualities, but as uncategorized concrete *persons*, then we must learn to make our primary identification of ourselves as persons and not distract our own consciousness by identifying ourselves through our social roles and class memberships.

It is true that biological and emotional attachments will continue to bind us, that social roles will continue to be exercised, and that on appropriate levels of our being we will continue to be "individual instances" of certain classes, just as our biological life will continue to be an information and energy exchange among cells composed of molecules made up of atoms. As members of these classes and functionaries of these roles, we will play our appointed parts—including rewriting the scripts. But it is not in this way that the creative union that makes the new creature comes about, for these roles and functions are always partial, not activating the whole of us, and comparatively superficial, not arising from the heart of us, therefore not our *characteristic* energy as human beings.

Here it is important to point out again that the energy that is the binding agent of the new creature is not emotional and to note, also, that the meaning shared is not merely factually informational. We can see this by comparing our vague dream of the human union with two forms of collective human organism with which we are already familiar: the crowd and the organization.

That a crowd of people will do things that no single one of them would do alone is well known, its consequences in lynch mobs, riots, and fanatical political-military states burned into our memories. Perhaps we are not equally aware of the same principle at work in religious crowds that are seized by the spirit invoked by their particular cult, in the excitement of crowds of sports fans, in audiences of popular musical stars.[7] What is going on here is that some primitive level of the human consciousness or subconsciousness is being aroused to move each element in the crowd so that the whole crowd behaves as a single living animal. The level of consciousness concerned is emotional and the entire body comes to be gripped by this shared emotion, which expresses itself in action—perhaps only singing, shouting, and dancing, with a little swooning or entrancement, but perhaps smashing, fire setting, and murdering.

The crowd flows about like an amoeba. Anyone can drop out of it, anyone can join it. No particular qualification is required, only an unquestioning yielding to the crowd's own character, which is its *feeling*. It has—*as* an emotional crowd—no internal structure. (In practice there is often a leader, and sometimes manipulating the crowd is an organization, but the organization as such and the crowd as such operate by distinct principles.)

A more benign type of collective human organism is the technological organization. Large businesses, governmental agencies, and scientific research and development teams are examples. Here the consciousness shared is rational. Data, information, patterns for relating the data, and directives for action are the operative linkages. There is no concern for the emotional qualities of the people involved in this type of linkage *as such*. Only factual information is exchanged; dispassionate objectivity is insisted upon.

The internal structure of the organization is detailed, even intricate, and usually rigid. The energy moves through channels and must stay in those channels regardless of how absurd (and sometimes even unjust and hurtful) this may be from a general human point of view. This collective animal does not flow about; it sits still and reaches out for its food, digests it, and puts forth its products and its wastes in an orderly fashion. It is able, like the crowd, to let its members go and to accept new ones, but now only on certain definite conditions. Anyone who has the requisite qualifications for a particular position in the organization may enter into it. If an element is lost from a position, it can be replaced by another element possessing the same qualifications.

The crowd corresponds to what I have called "paleo-feminine" consciousness, a wholistic, emotional, flowing, unreflective state of being. The organization corresponds to what, in that scheme, was called "masculism," a rationalistic reflective consciousness that divides its subject matter, specializes, focuses, arranges, puts in rank ordering of superior and inferior, and ends by becoming domineering and mechanistic. The third state of consciousness, towards which we are now groping, can be expected to be a "neo-feminism," again a wholistic, generalist, unifying state of being, but one that has absorbed the benefits of internal differentiation and reflective consciousness. In addition, it will have passed beyond both emotionalism and rationalism to an even clearer and more integrated consciousness that we may point to[8] by calling it intellectual intuition and creative love.

"Intuition" says that it reaches a concrete being as its goal and does so without mediation, while "intellectual" says that it does this consciously, knowing what it does and how. "Creative love" indicates that this consciousness does not so much passively know other beings as they already are and have been, and respond affectively to the values they already have, as it actively projects being towards others. It is creative in its intention to share life. It moves to make something new for the future. It sees the reality of the other's being, especially as it may be, as it shall be, and it wills the goodness of the other, that it may be, that it shall be. In order that this future may actually come to pass, the one identifying with this creative consciousness pours living self-being into the other. In a community formed by this type of consciousness, the energy and meaning exchanged among the members are the self-realization and the self-giving love that are the very selfhood and existence of the members, the knowing, the willing, and the loving being all one integral act of a unified faculty with a creative orientation and motivation.

The communal organism united by this consciousness will not stream about like a crowd, nor ingest and produce like an organization. It will radiate being-goodness in an unceasing circulating mutual indwelling, like the Trinity. Its internal structure will be that paradox for rationalistic consciousness of the coincidence of unity and multiplicity. The whole being of each member will be shared with all, with the consequence that each will become both the whole and absolutely unique. Can anyone enter or leave this collective organism, as they could the crowd or the organization? No. Everyone must belong to it and no one can leave. This is true in the sense that this is the principle of the organism's being, this is the way it is constructed, the kind of being it is. It cannot be the being it is to be unless all persons are incorporated into it. Because each of its elements is absolutely unique, it cannot afford to lose any. It cannot replace a missing member with another having the same qualifications. Not all the remaining elements could compensate it for the loss of even a single one.[9]

A major concern of the organism, therefore, and thus of all its constituent elements, must be to prize, protect, nurture, and promote each element in its unique personhood. Each center of spondic energy in this living body will realize that it most literally is loving its neighbor as its self and that whatever it does to any member it does to the whole[10] and, thereby, to every member, including itself.

How would such a consciousness work out in practice, we want to ask. What kinds of economic systems, what political forms, what social and familial relationships would it spawn? We cannot know exactly, because one of the conditions of this consciousness is that it must always develop in the concrete. We cannot work out by abstract reasoning what its characteristics will be. We can take only one step at a time, *beginning from the inside*, and discover in living experience the new creature. An entire attitude, mind-set, way of identifying self and others and perceiving the world has to shift *first*, before any talk of economic, political, and social arrangements can be anything but premature, useless, and possibly dangerous.

A few negative remarks may be possible. Whatever form the outward manifestation of the new creature will take, it must not conflict with the internal structure, that is, with the exchange of spondic energy. Each member is essentially a radiating center and must not be encouraged to become a gravitational center, to suck being into itself. When we love another person, we must will that that person become an overflowing source of spondic energy. We are not to will that the person have sensual pleasures, emotional satisfactions, wealth and power, fame and influence, or any number of things that we now imagine constitute "abundant life." We are not to will that one be deprived of these things, either. The point is that these are no longer the cardinal values, the ones on which our sense of well-being is hinged.

Another important point is that the world developed under the guidance of this *perichoretic* consciousness will not be homogeneous. Everyone is to be loved equally, but every one is unique. People will not identify themselves in terms of the classes to which they belong, but this need not mean that ethnic and cultural diversity should disappear from our society. Perhaps the diversity will increase to the point where each person is an ethnic culture unto himself, delighted in by all his equally diverse companions. We must remember that the principle of this kind of being is essentially the coexistence and co-valuation of unity and multiplicity.

Although we cannot lay out the precise structure of a world whose paradigm is *perichoresis*, we can probably see what the next step must be from where we stand now. It is that each of us practice, in whatever way we find most efficacious, to realize ourselves as transcendent spondic energy and to perceive others in the same way. When this becomes a real spontaneous perception, not just an ideal set before the imagination, but the *obvious* way in which we orient ourselves, then we will also spontaneously behave in terms of this perception, just as we now spontaneously behave in terms of our perception of ourselves as separated, selfish, class-identified, needy creatures, who are consequently often greedy and untrustworthy.

When some of us do perceive ourselves and others this way, will the others stop being greedy and untrustworthy? No, not until they also really identify themselves with their transcendent spondic selves, and in the meantime their neighbors will have to take sensible protective measures. This is not a transition that is going to come quickly, and while the transition is going on, we must use common sense. But the slowness should not discourage us, either, or cause us to exclaim that we cannot change human nature, that people will always be selfish at bottom, no matter how altruistic they may appear in their better moments. Like all great shifts in evolution, this projected elevation of our consciousness can be expected to be a massive, radical transformation that, while it is a kind of "quantum leap" in each individual in whom it happens, shows up in whole populations only very gradually over a long period of time.

The advantage that we have with *this* evolutionary shift, however, is that we now (we think) understand something of how evolution works in general and which way it is moving, so that we can consciously help. Indeed, if the next step is such as described here, initiated by a self-realization as transcendent spondic energy, it cannot possibly take place at all *except* by our conscious participation. The evolutionary step *consists of* a certain free and conscious act on our part.

It is a peculiar situation, in which we feel that the pressure of all of nature's own tendency to develop is back of us, pushing us to go forward in a particular way, and yet this very going forward has to be a free act on our part. If it is not free, it just is not the act that is needed at this point.

We cannot require people to love one another, and trying to coerce them to act as if they did, does not work satisfactorily, for it seems to breed the very hostilities it sets out to contain. We have resorted to exhortation, persuasion, enticement, encouragement. But these methods have not been very successful, either. So let us try *understanding*. Perhaps if we can clearly grasp with our intelligent consciousness—our seeing-valuing power—what kind of being we profoundly are and something of what we may become, we will be able to experience that miraculous gestalt shift, that *metanoia*, that *satori*, that turns the world inside out and transvalues all the values.

Notes

1. "The Holy Thursday Revolution," *Liturgy* (July 1978).

2. "Neo-Feminism as Communion Consciousness," *Anima* (Fall 1978); "Humanity in the Image of the Trinitarian God," *Prabuddha Bharata* (March 1979).

3. Cf. Exod. 3:14 and Gen. 1:3.

4. Cf. Matt. 8:20. Having worked through the experience itself and developed the argument in its own terms, we may now recall odd fragments of scripture and wonder whether something like this was what was meant there.

5. *The New Catholic Encyclopedia* article on "Circumincession" (by A. M. Bermejo), speaking of the Greek conception of the Trinity, says: "It is a 'reciprocal irruption' (Cyril of Alexandria) or unceasing circulation of life. Thus, each person being necessarily in the other two, unity is achieved not so much on account of the unicity of a single passive nature but rather because of this irresistible impulse in each person, which mightily draws them to one another."

6. Pierre Teilhard de Chardin, *The Phenomenon of Man* (New York: Harper, 1959), p. 57 et passim.

7. For examples, see William Sargant, *The Mind Possessed: A Physiology of Possession, Mysticism and Faith Healing* (Philadelphia: Lippincott, 1974).

8. In the sense in which Zen Buddhism insists that all its utterances are only "fingers pointing at the moon" of the experience itself. Following the direction of the finger, you get a hint, but to see the moon, you must look for yourself.

9. Cf. Luke 15:4.

10. Cf. Matt. 25:40.

FIVE

Trinitarian Personhood

Sometimes our efforts to analyze ourselves as persons, particularly when we do an existential or metaphysical analysis, seem rather esoteric and far removed from daily life and the immediacy of human evil and suffering. Yet I believe it is only this kind of analysis that will effectively prepare us for the release and transformation we seek. Over the centuries people have tried preaching, exhorting, threatening, and promising, even tried setting a good example (which is the best way), but without *explanations* sufficiently profound, clear, and convincing, these methods have been limited in their power to achieve the desired goal. Therefore it seems to me that we must continue struggling to understand ourselves, as a first step in the struggle to transform ourselves.

In this chapter I explore the mystery of personhood, what it is and how it relates to human nature. The suggestion is that if we reflect on the Trinity and interpret it in a certain way, it can serve as a paradigm that helps us understand ourselves in community. There are two main themes, dependent on one another: how unity and plurality coexist and what freely extended self-sharing, or love, is. This will involve some curious things being said about "grace," about an "I-I" relation that lies one step beyond the "I-Thou" relation, and about an "ecstasy-enstasy circle."

After that I make some remarks about the distinction of this personhood from our human nature and what can be expected from each in an effort to improve our lives. In conclusion, some guidelines are offered for what we might try to do if the scheme seems to fit.

Ourselves as Persons in the Image of the Trinity

The first point is to gain some sense of ourselves as persons in the image of the Trinity. That is, I want to explore the consequences of supposing that it is not merely that we are made in the image of *God*, but expressly in the image of the *Trinity*.

When we draw attention to the Trinity as such, as distinguished from just speaking of God, we are pointing to some kind of internal differentiation. This differentiation or distinction is technically represented in terms of "generation" and "spiration" and, more popularly, in terms of personal relations of knowing and loving. Something approaching "plurality" is being indicated but simultaneously denied. We speak of three Persons in one God. Here we may notice that insofar as there is any suggestion of anything approaching "plurality," it always has reference to the Persons, not to the nature of God.

Perhaps there is something about personhood that requires a kind of plurality that can also be denied. That is the idea that I am going to develop. Person is not the kind of being that can exist, or even be conceived, in singularity. We must always think *persons*, plural. Therefore, when we say "we" as persons are made in the image of God, and God is Trinity, we must mean "we, taken all together," not "each of us, taken severally." Being taken together, not severed, must be essential to being persons. *Persons are a plurality that is also a unity.*

When we look for the image of God in ourselves, then, let us look at our community. It may be that it is not possible (has no meaning) to find the image of God in *myself*, singular. Just as God does not (cannot) exist as only one Person, so we are the image not as singulars alone but as the community. As the image of the Holy Trinity, we are, in our deepest reality, the Holy Community.

A second point to note about our personal existence in image of the Trinity is the emphasis on activity and process, the sense of movement and flow, rather than an emphasis on definition of a static kind of being. Trinitarianism is not just the coexistence of unity and plurality. Whatever "generation," "spiration," and "love" may mean, they seem to point to some essential self-giving *activity*. The Divine Persons share the divine life by freely communicating it to one another, and that activity of giving and sharing is what primarily constitutes their life. In fact, the very unity of the Godhead is not to be regarded as something that is there from the outset as "achieved" by these free personal acts of self-sharing. No, it is not even what is "achieved." It just *is* the process of the giving and sharing, in which the sharing is so profound, so total, that each Person thoroughly indwells or lives in each other Person, and that is what makes the unity.

Persons Are a Plurality Whose Action Makes a Unity

Similarly, our reality as persons is found in our doing, not in the sense of getting something *done*—that is not the point—but in the sense of the present living moment of process. Each member of the person-community is a sheer "I am," beyond anything that can be said *about* me, beyond any descriptive attributes that can be predicated *of* me. I am simply my process, my activity. But what activity? This same naked "I am" is, simultaneously and equally, basically a radiant "May you be"—that is, the will (and the act) to extend being and life. This is why it is persons, or more properly the activity that persons are, and not nature, that constitutes the unity of the Trinity and the unity of our Holy Community.

This is important to grasp, because we tend to think and to imagine that reality is basically a set of separate inert substances and that activity is later, is something that substances do (or perhaps don't do) as an accident, and has the consequence of establishing relations between the substances. What the paradigm of the Trinity shows us is that the activity itself is the basic reality on which all else depends.

One further consideration follows. If I am my process, then I am not to be reduced to, and equated with, what I have done. I am a "living one," continuously creating my action. Insofar as my action is profoundly free and proceeds only from me as person, there is no way to predict it. It is truly creative. This is true of every member of the person-community. If we are to be together in love and self-sharing, then we will have to give ourselves to one another in trust.

The third point I would note here is that love is a very special kind of act and relation, for it establishes at one and the same time, and by a single act, both unity and differentiation. As a lover, I must give myself to "another" in order to be a lover; this is differentiation. But by the act of self-giving, union is achieved. This is what makes the Trinity to be the Trinity: *the Persons are a plurality that is necessarily a unity*. And this is the crucial value for us as persons if we are to realize ourselves in the image of the Trinity. For this self-giving, or exchange of being and life, that we commonly call "love" is, I want to urge, the defining characteristic of persons: in this activity lives the reality of personhood.

Freedom and Grace

Self-giving is the central point in our talk about love and personhood. What do we mean by it? Sometimes, in human relations, it means to give time, attention, emotional response, intelligence, creative skills, and bodily activity for another person's benefit. Sometimes it means to sacrifice one's material life in order to save another. It can also mean to procreate and to nourish and to teach. In general, it seems to mean to give what one considers oneself to *be*, as distinguished from what one *has*, to give what cannot be *separated from* oneself: in order to give it, you yourself have to go along and be present—you can't send it by messenger. As a personal act, it means that all our conscious faculties are involved: knowing and understanding what we are doing, willing the welfare of the other, feeling appropriate affections toward the other, appreciating the values involved in the whole situation.

If it is truly self-giving, the act must obviously be free. Ordinarily we think of freedom in the context of making choices: the environment sets up various alternatives for us and then puts pressure on us in some way to make a choice among them. Even the choice between acting and not acting is of this type. When we make the choice, it is a reaction to what the environment has offered. For instance, we see someone who is beautiful and good, who embodies the highest moral values and performs heroic deeds. We *react* to this person with love, approbation, praise, admiration, and so on. These are splendid affections on our part, thoroughly commendable. Nevertheless, they are instances of reaction and choice freedom. In this case the act of love does not originate purely in the one who loves, but really arises in the environment as the lovability of the one who is loved.

Fine as this kind of love is, there is a self-giving that exceeds it, in which the lover is the absolute first source of love that issues in creative freedom. Creative freedom is something more than choice freedom. It is not a re-action to something in the environment, based on the nature and the value of that object. It is not a *re*-action at all. It is an original *first* action. There is not only no determinism, no compulsion, no necessity of nature to force the act; there is not even any overwhelming motivation originating in the object of love or elsewhere in the environment. The lover acts out of creative freedom, which precedes any estimation of the value of the beloved.

Thus the creative lover does not love the beloved because the beloved is lovable or deserving—or because the beloved is undeserving. There is no "because" anywhere that would answer "why" the creative lover loves by pointing to some reality outside the loving act itself as a sufficient reason for the love: not because the lover hopes for a reward from a third party, not because there is an internal need or one "can't help it," or even that it is the "nature" of the lover to do so.

The act of loving is a *personal* act, not the act of a nature. It is called "creative" because it arises out of nothing, not having any predecessor in its own order. And for all these reasons, this love is an act of *grace*. Grace is the free, unmerited gift of a benefit, especially an act of self-giving. We are used to thinking of it in terms of gifts from God to us, especially the gift of sharing the divine life itself. But having received the gift of divine life, surely we then actually live it, and this must mean that we are to make such gifts ourselves. We are also to extend our life to one another by grace.

It may seem strange to use the word this way, but I am going to suggest that even when we love God, it is an act of grace in this sense. St. Augustine has said that the saint is one who seeks to love God *not for any reason*. That is to say (in my view), it is our original, free act of self-giving. And that is grace. If this may be rightly said, then we here gaze on a great mystery: that the interpersonal communion between ourselves as free persons and God is so profound that we may not only receive grace from God but may give grace to God.

But all these acts of grace, we may suppose, are reflections of the intense life of self-giving, of life-sharing, within the Trinity itself. If it is not wrong to say that in the Holy Trinity the divine life is shared by the three Persons because they communicate it to one another— that is, divine life *is* the activity of unmotivated self-sharing—if this is not wrong to say, then the very heart of the divine life itself is *grace:* personal offering in original creative freedom. This is precisely what that life consists of: the act of personal offering, the free giving and receiving, the exchange, the circulation, the *circumincession*, of personal life.

My contention is that this Trinitarian movement is the revelation and the paradigm of all personal reality. Persons are those who engage in this activity of self-giving in love by grace, by creative freedom. I will note here, for development later, that if we do not engage in the behaviors that incarnate love by creative freedom, that is, by grace acting as persons, but try to perform them out of our nature, by motivation from the environment under choice freedom, we will usually experience difficulty, and in any case, we will not yet be doing the *divine* thing. Grace is the identifying characteristic of divine life, whether within the Trinity itself, between the Trinity and us, or among ourselves as persons.

The Karma Trap and the Problem of Evil

All this casts an interesting light on the problem of suffering. There are several points to be discussed: One, the order of nature is the order of action and reaction, including choice freedom, and is to be distinguished from the order of creative freedom, which is the order of the person and divine life. Evil and suffering are found in the order of nature. Two, as long as we lodge our sense of identity and our significant acts and experiences in the order of nature alone, we are caught in what I will call the Karma Trap, and we will characterize our life as suffering. Three, when we transcend the order of reaction and choice freedom to act in the order of creative freedom, then we perform the characteristic divine act and live the divine life.

The first point: In the order of nature the various beings interact with one another according to their natures. Sufficiently energetic particles split atomic nuclei; atoms with matching valences bond to form molecules; RNA molecules monitor the synthesis of proteins; antibodies destroy foreign organisms; wasps sting and paralyze caterpillars; monkeys groom one another. All of these are feedback systems; to every such action there is a re-action.

Among human beings, our social behavior is a complicated fabric of reaction patterns. Almost everything that we do is done as a response of some kind to something already in our environment. That includes such free acts as selecting what we will have for dinner and deciding to rob the local convenience store. It covers the sharp word we speak and our failure to take on charitable efforts, deciding to situate our factory where labor is cheap and continuing to do research on biological weapons. We make choices, and each of these choices has been presented to us by the environment and conditioned by our past experience, just as the choice itself, once enacted, will become part of the public environment for ourselves and others and will condition both them and us for our next piece of behavior. This is a chain and a network of reactions.

It is my contention that all the evil that we do and all our suffering falls in this order of reaction and choice freedom. There is also good here, of course. But evil, unlike good, *has* to be here if anywhere, because it has to operate relatively. Good can stand without reference and can originate an act from nothing, can operate in the realm of creative freedom, but evil always has to be referred to other beings and to operate as a reaction, or choice, not as an original creative act that simply rises up from nothing. There are always reasons why we do evil, even if they are very complex, difficult to bring to the surface, and almost unrelated to the obvious features of the public act. There is no such thing as unmotivated evildoing, as a parallel to unmotivated love. Good and evil are not equal and opposite, reciprocals, or two poles of a single spectrum.

Suffering is both the direct pain of injury on some level and the will that this should not be. Suffering can be vicarious because we can also will that others should not experience pain or injustice. This com-passion, like our responses to beauty and goodness, can be a very high act, and I do not want to say that these are not personal acts. Personal acts of creative freedom can be embodied in natural acts and manifested as responses. But responses to the distress of others can also come out of our own discomfort in their presence and our desire for our own relief. In this case, we also are caught in the reaction pattern. Creative freedom is operative when one is not caught in the reaction pattern but affectively unites with the sufferer and wills the release from pain without any motive that has reference to oneself.

This is the second point, that as long as we limit our experience, our sense of selfhood, and our interior and exterior acts to the order of nature—the order of reaction and choice freedom—*alone*, we will continue to go round and round in the circle I call the Karma Trap. We will react to this situation and then react to our own reaction and to others' reactions to our reaction, and so on. All our acts will be compensations, efforts to balance or pacify or neutralize some unbalanced situation. Every act will overshoot and cause another imbalance, which will call forth other attempts, on our part and the part of others, to correct the matter. Our physiological life is like that, our small-scale social behaviors are like that, and so are our large-scale political interactions.

I am not saying that this is necessarily bad. Indeed, by this means the whole machinery of embodied life moves forward. But I am saying that this is not in itself *personal* activity and that the way out of suffering cannot be found on this level. The essence of suffering, we might say, is to be trapped on this level, unable to do anything *except* react to whatever the environment (including things that go on in our own bodies and psyches) puts up. I think that this may be close to what the First Noble Truth of Buddhism is saying: natural life is suffering.

However, our third point, like the Buddhists' Third Noble Truth, says that there is a way out. When we transcend the order of reaction and choice freedom, to act in the order of creative freedom, then we perform the characteristic divine act and live the divine life. Notice that what makes an act of creative freedom free is just that it is not a reaction, a response to a previously existing situation or value. One who acts out of creative freedom becomes impartial as God is impartial, who makes the sun rise on the evil and on the good and sends rain on the just and on the unjust (Matt. 5:43–48). It is in doing this that our divine filiation is verified. God is like this; this is the sort of thing that God does. When we do it, we are doing a divine act and behaving as children of God, those who have received, and who live by, the life of God.

We are to love our enemies as we love our neighbors, pray for those who persecute us as we pray for our benefactors. The point is to be *impartial*, that is to say, we are to love them not because of their behavior *either way*. We are not to love them *because* they are our enemies, any more than we are to love them *because* they are our friends. This means, of course, that we cannot advert to the fact that it is an "enemy" that we are loving and congratulate ourselves on our virtue. We have to transcend the label of "enemy." That means that we have to strip off, both from ourselves and from that other, all those attributes and past behaviors that made up the action-reaction pattern in which we and they could be labeled mutual "enemies." This stripping may have to go so deep that there is nothing left on either side but the sheer "I am" of the person, beyond anything in the natural order.

That is the experience that the Sermon on the Mount is trying to drive us to, the Narrow Door that the Good Shepherd would herd us through, because this is the deep truth of what and who we are; and it is the realization of this truth that will set us free from evil and suffering.

The Ecstasy and the Enstasy

Now I want to examine a little more closely this gracious act of self-giving, this going out from oneself into the other, that unmotivated love is. I describe this as a personal act in which all the faculties are unified: it is knowing and willing and imagining and feeling, or affectivity, all integrated. It is to be found as complete and total giving in the personal relationship I call "I-I."

This is a step beyond the familiar "I-Thou" relation, which we distinguish from the "I-It." In the I-It relation, we as subject relate to an object as object. This object is regarded as not having a personal presence of its own, not being an origin of free acts. We operate as though we are the only personal consciousness there, and our consciousness—knowing, willing, loving—reflects off the object and returns to us. We experience nothing whatever of the object's own interiority, its selfhood. The object has no "face" for us. It is possible to relate to human beings this way, but we protest against it because it fails to recognize the reality that is there.

We correct this error when we shift to I-Thou. Now we are "face to face," we say. Whereas we had talked *about* an "it," we speak *to* a "thou." One personal consciousness confronts another personal consciousness, acknowledging that it is another personal consciousness, capable of its own free acts. Each responds to the other in dialogue. In this way we receive something of the other's interior selfhood, because the other tells us about it and we listen, take it into ourself. But what we receive is mediated, translated into the medium of communication, encoded. We receive it through images, concepts, tones, glances, gestures, which we have to translate back into what we hope are comparable memories from our own experience. In this sense, although we acknowledge that we are dealing with another subject, it is still as an object (where "subject" and "object" are taken grammatically). The other is someone whom we can know and love, even as we can be known and loved by the other, but into whose own subjective reality we do not enter.

If we are to relate to the other subject truly as subject, then we cannot "confront" the other. We cannot *look at* the other, or *listen to* the other, or *speak to* the other. These interactions, which had been such an improvement over the I-It relation, are still not intimate enough. The goal of love, which is complete and total giving, as well as the goal of knowledge, is union. This is why the mystics say that the union takes place in darkness—nothing is *seen* as object—and in silence—one does not *listen* or *speak*, because the self-revelation is not mediated. We must enter into the other and experience what the other experiences *as* the other experiences it. Instead of being "face to face," the two faces are superimposed, so to speak, both facing the same way, so that they look out through coinciding eyes and speak through coinciding lips. The activities of the two subjectivities are confluent and simultaneous, instead of being responsive, alternating, as in dialogue. Each of them knows the other from the inside, from the subject side, in terms of the experience of actually doing what that subject does. And each totally loves the other by uniting with the other in this complete way.

This is the genuine ecstasy, the passing *out* of oneself to enter into the other, there to be *as* the other. This is the goal of the mystical life, according to all mystical traditions, the nondual state in which the duality of subject and object has been transcended and the mystic so enters into God's subjectivity as to share that divine life from the inside, to experience it as God experiences it. This could be our understanding of the Trinitarian life itself, that the Divine Persons relate to one another in an "I-I" relation, each passing fully into the subjective activity of each other, in that mutual indwelling and coinherence that we call *perichoresis* or *circumincession*.

And this could be our understanding of ourselves, of the characteristic reality of personhood and, therefore, of our origin and of our destiny. For, I would suggest, we come forth from God in precisely an I-I relation. God's ecstatic movement *is* our personal selfhood. We are constituted as persons by this I-I relation in which God knows/loves in coincidence with us. The mystical union which we look toward as the *goal* of our life is the same relation, seen from our point of view, as our *origin*, which is God's mystical union with us.

It is important to note that our "I," our personhood, is not a *product* of God's action, something left over after the action has ceased. Rather it *is* God's action in the very actuality of acting. "We" are not a thing but an activity. This is why God's activity of ecstatically moving out to us is an act of coinciding with our activity, just as our union with God will be our ecstatically moving out to God as an act of coinciding with God's activity. This is also why it is only the naked "I am," transcending all the descriptive attributes of one's nature and history, that can perform the ecstatic act.

This activity which we are and which God is, is the act of creative freedom, of initiative, of self-originated self-giving. This is what we fundamentally *are* as persons, just as it is what God is as personal. So when we come into being as our experience of God's union with us, or when we attain our destiny as our experience of our union with God, what is happening in both cases is that two self-giving activities are confluent.

Since the reality of person is a *free* act of self-giving, this act cannot be said to be *caused*. The person is not "contingent" in the usual sense. In the view I am offering, we as persons arise in God's mystical union with our acts of free personal self-giving. You can't think this with a temporal beginning, and you can't think it with a logical beginning according to which the person should first *be there*, and then place its free act, and then the other person enters into it. No, what enables the person to *be there* in the first place is just that this "other person" *does* enter into the first person. The argument comes round in a circle. I think that this is part of what is involved in being in the image of the Trinity.

Notice another strange circle. Person *is* the act of acting personally. This is the act of self-giving. A person will act ecstatically by entering through self-giving into another person's subjectivity and join there in that one's activity. But when that union is realized, the lover knows the beloved as the beloved experiences self-knowing. This experience of self-knowing we call *enstasy*, profound standing *in* oneself. Thus by ecstasy the lover enters into the beloved's own enstatic self-realization.

But what is this profound self-realization? It is the realization that one is a naked "I am" that is simultaneously a "May you be," for one is a person, that is, a lover, that is, one who goes out in ecstasy to a beloved. So ecstasy means that one enters into and unites with another's enstasy, which is *that one's* own act of ecstasy toward still another, in which act it unites with that further one's enstasy.

The only way it can be manifested that two persons really have united—and in fact the only way that such union can take place—is by their acting together as a single actor; that is, together they must love still another person, must project themselves outward toward another in ecstasy. Having so projected themselves into the I-I relation with the third person, they and the third person will be in a common enstasy, the proof (equals actuality) of which will be that the enstatic trio will act as one in a further act of ecstatic love toward yet another, with whom they will unite in enstasy, and so on.

The structure of this pattern does not really change beyond the number three; for three acting as one to project toward a fourth is not formally different from two ecstatically turned toward the third. That the first two should unite in their ecstatic movement toward the third is necessary as the actuality of their own union. Therefore three is the minimum and the sufficient number to display, and to act as the paradigm for, the structure of the process. Besides, the process must come full circle: the first person must also be the "recipient," so to speak, of the ecstatic love of at least two others, who, acting as one, unite with that "first" in enstasy.

We can see—if this view has any validity—that foundational being, personal being, is a free process that simultaneously maintains differentiation and union. The act of love is what protects us from solipsism, in spite of the fact that it also establishes nonduality. The act of ecstasy verifies differentiation, but when ecstasy is successful in its intent to enter thoroughly into the other by complete and total giving, then it becomes that other's own enstasy and thus perfect union is also verified. This seems to me to be *the* characteristic act of persons who exist in the image of the Trinity.

The Persons We Are Struggling to Realize

This is the insight structure I have to offer. Can it be of any practical benefit with respect to the world of affliction? I believe that clarifying the distinction between person and nature would help. We are used to thinking of ourselves as individuals, separate and different instances of human nature, differentiated by mutually exclusive attributes: you can tell us apart by some combination of qualities that each one has and no one else possesses. This, we fondly believe, is what makes us "unique" and *therefore valuable*. There is no one else "just like me." But these supposedly precious qualities, as possessions (not what one *is* but what one *has*), are contingent and vulnerable. They have to be protected in order to be maintained. I think it is because we have confused the true person (the act of loving) with this individualized instance of nature (a bundle of possessed attributes) that we are always so troubled by insecurity, the fear and pain of losing our attributes, and consequently by the host of defensive and offensive attitudes and behaviors we have constructed to cope with these threats.

I think further that, having reduced the person to the individual, we then imposed upon the individual the obligation to do certain things that only a person can do. When the individual failed to do these things, we blamed and punished the individual, who consequently experienced guilt but was not thereby enabled to stop failing. In the end, we made a mystique out of our failure, elevating it to the dignity of sin, the crowning proof of our freedom, when the whole thing was really a *mistake*, the mistake of not finding ourselves as who we truly are.

It seems very clear to me that what we have to do is stop encouraging people to identify only with their natures and, instead, support one another in our struggle to realize ourselves as persons. Human nature, like any other nature, is going to act to protect and augment itself, that is, selfishly and egotistically. That's its nature. That's what it's *supposed* to do, because only in this way can it secure its differentiation and establish itself in being. It's not like the person, whose differentiation is secured precisely by giving itself away. Differentiation in the order of nature is attained by organizing goods around oneself. We ought not to be surprised or offended when we observe the natural order behaving this way.

We are a mysterious being. The myth of the Incarnate God is the myth of us all. We are a union of the personal and the natural, the divine and the human. We have all the directed energies of human nature proper to its own order, and we also have insights and aspirations pertaining to the personal order. We want to live the self-giving life of the person in the order of nature, and we blame ourselves when we cannot do so. We are particularly distressed because we do not merely fail to live up to the high ideals of the personal order, but we even do extraordinarily cruel and wicked things to one another that do not seem to be accounted for by some simple reference to "the drives of human nature."

But, then, the goals of *human* nature are not so simple. They are, in fact, extremely complex. They include subtle things, such as the sense of satisfaction in paying an enemy back (the ego's sense of justice and vindication of dignity), complicated compensation systems for a multitude of obscure psychological hurts and inadequacies, the need for peer approval and self-approbation, the desire to create structures, control events and people, have the power of making and breaking. All of these are manifestations of the need to establish ourselves in being and differentiation of *human nature*, which, elevated as it is above merely vegetative and animal nature, is nevertheless not the same as the personal order. Just being immaterial isn't the same as being personal.

These desires of human nature and the actions that arise from them are part of the reaction net that I called the Karma Trap. Many of these actions cause affliction, and many of them have themselves arisen out of the experience of being afflicted and needing to balance or neutralize or compensate for the pain. This is the realm in which the various behavior codes of humanity are framed and in which choice freedom moves to turn perceptions and feelings into action.

When we try to improve that human-nature world out of the motives and the dynamisms available *in* it, we don't get very far. What can we show? It is true that human nature is intensely gregarious and communitarian. We are endlessly interdependent, not only economically but intellectually and emotionally, and this interdependence increases exponentially as our culture advances. It is also true that our human nature craves fellowship, yearns for someone to talk to who will listen sympathetically, for someone to take care of us when we are in need, and even for someone or something that we may succor, because that makes us feel "useful" and "needed." We need to do "good deeds" in order to feel comfortable with ourselves, because we have internalized a moral code that holds this up as an ideal. Often it turns out that it is our self-image that is at stake. Our very sense of pride, our self-approbation, requires us to behave as if we are humble and generous. In such ways is the fabric of our society knitted together: each thread goes out and loops through other threads and then returns to itself, drawing others around it. All of these strange, complex, involuted needs and desires of ours do in fact produce a kind of working union. But *what* kind of union is it? I call it an imitation.

By means of a little limited altruism—mostly restricted to families or co-religionists or compatriots—together with a good deal of stimulation of pride and greed, and large quantities of fear, we have managed to put together a weak and wobbly facsimile of a community. But a balancing off of selfishnesses, an unstable equilibrium of egotisms, even if it does not corrode into crime or explode into war, is not yet real life-sharing, is not true love, is not genuine community, is not the Holy Community of our ideal vision. And it is not to be expected that it should be. *Human nature cannot save itself.* Its redemption has to come to it from above, from the order of the personal.

I think the reason why we find it so hard to take our place in the Great Community is just because we have not clearly sorted out which motives and energies come from human nature and which movements must come from the person, and we keep trying to perform essentially divine acts—such as loving everyone, even our enemies, as ourselves—out of the resources of our human psychologies, which are quite inadequate for such marvels. Human nature does not fail herein to do something that it ought to be able to do. The principle of its structure as a nature does not enable it to do such things.

Every being has to strive to remain in being, to differentiate or elaborate itself in being. Human natures are differentiated by the drive to organize goods—including intellectual and emotional goods—around themselves. Only the *person* is so structured that it secures its being, differentiation, and expansion by going out from itself and giving itself to others. Therefore, the only way we can come to the ideal life to which we aspire is by first going to the transcendent level of the person and *then* incarnating the person in the human soul and body. But now a new principle of organization must order our perceptions, our feelings, our behaviors. This is the "new heart" of which Ezekiel speaks (18:31; cf. 11:19), a new center of life and activity; it is the "new nature, created after the likeness of God in true righteousness and holiness" of the Epistle to the Ephesians (4:24).

How can we go to the transcendent level of the person? First, we have to think through the difference between nature and person, so that we have a clear idea of where the confusion has arisen. We need especially to elaborate the structure of personal life, as for instance I tried to do with the description of the I-I relation and the ecstatic-enstatic circle. This gives us some kind of initial orientation as to what sort of thing we are trying to do. But then we must *experience* personal being with all our conscious faculties, we must *realize* it with intellect, will, imagination, affectivity, and action.

We may be helped by the gracious touch of someone who is already living according to the personal principle and who can therefore relate to us in unmotivated love in such a way that we actually experience it. This will be an I-I relation and will awaken in *us* the "I" that is capable of the I-I relations. Someone who *is* free can set others free (cf. John 8:36: "If the Son makes you free, you will be free indeed"), and then they in turn can free still others ("Freely you have received, freely give," Matt. 10:8). I like to call this a "Savior chain." In any case, the internal Savior is God, who is always relating to each of us by the I-I relation as the foundation of our very existence. By deep meditation we may find the place in ourselves where God is loving us into existence. When that happens, our eyes will be opened so that we can perceive being in the personal realm. We will be able to look at someone and see the *person*, not just the individual collection of nature attributes, and seeing the person, we will be able really to move out to that person in self-sharing love.

Meanwhile, we can implement what insight we have by starting to revise the words and actions of daily life, considering how almost everything in our culture tends to confuse the person with the individual of nature. I think that we need to analyze the cultural forms of our daily life and to make changes to new cultural forms, which we will devise. These behavioral changes will work in a circle with our meditation, each helping each, until both become familiar and easy.

To sum up, I see these general guidelines growing out of our discussion of the person in terms of the Trinitarian, ecstatic life:

One, we must get used to perceiving ourselves and others as persons who transcend their human nature; that is, we must give up reducing people to individuals whom we can locate, label, and evaluate in terms of their attributes, possessions, positions, and past deeds. This is the meaning of forgiveness and divine impartiality. This also implies relating to other people in terms of faith, that is, being willing to be engaged with or committed to them, realizing that we do not know what they will do next.

Two, we must learn to be comfortable with the sense of our reality and our value being in our process, not in our substance; that is, not in our possessions or products, or in our successes or failures. This means, among other things, that our whole attitude toward time must change: insofar as we are in time, our reality is in our momentariness, and we should learn to savor the present, rather than live artificially in the past or the future.

Three, we must allow ourselves to have a real sense of ourselves as a community. It is all of us together who are in the image of the Trinity. There is no such thing as just one person. That is a metaphysical impossibility. We are all, necessarily, profoundly with everyone else on the personal level. You can never think of yourself as only yourself. Because of the compounding of the I-I relations in the total community, all persons are involved in you and you are involved in all of them.

Four, we should practice trying to perform unmotivated acts: do each thing in the thing's own terms, for its own sake, not for the sake of the product or the achievement or the reward. Especially, we should relax our emotions and leave ourselves free to offer unmotivated love to other persons.

If these habits of thought and feeling could become so deeply embedded in us that we automatically operated by them without effort, without questioning, without adverting to them, then we would be in a position to alleviate the afflictions of the world.

SIX

The Whole World

A Convergence Perspective

We must realize, said Teilhard de Chardin, that *"we are evolution."*[1] The rising tide of material complexity and centered consciousness has doubled back on itself; it has become reflexive in our capacity to know and to construct. We are the being that knows that it knows and that makes tools for making tools. The erstwhile simple energies of evolution have become compound in us, and we have become the being in which psychic energy has attained "consciousness of the second degree."[2] This elevation and self-possession finds its apex in what is at once both our most glorious and our most dreaded quality: our freedom. No more is there an innate instinct whose wisdom works through our sleeping souls to build us marvelous dwellings of shells or webs or combs or nests, to guide us unerringly on long journeys, to direct us to procure our proper diet. No more is there a routinized response to every stimulus, a tidy playback of well-established habits governing the daily activities of individual and tribe. No more will the evolutionary forces of nature propel us in their groping way through the next critical point into a new state of being. From now on, if we are to have any future, *we must create that future ourselves*.

We reflexive consciousnesses know a little about freedom and about creation. We know that creation means standing on the boundary between being and nonbeing and stepping into the abyss of nothingness. We know that freedom means taking responsibility for the kind of world that forms under our feet as we take that decisive step.

But who can bear to make the great decisions? To face the terrifying glory of creative freedom? The very prospect appalls us. Little decisions we can handle: what to have for dinner, what book to read, which job to take, whose political party to endorse. But—how to set the course of civilization by shaping our own consciousness and the consciousness of others; whether to continue with conventional social attitudes; what religion to adopt; how to bring up children—give us back our routines, something in us implores. Leave us our habits, our traditions, our good old days when the tracks were laid out for us and we could slide down them with a minimum of consciousness. As Walter Kaufmann has so aptly said,[3] we are suffering from "decidophobia." We are all too willing that Someone Else should make the great decisions. Let our spouse do it, we urge, or our institution, or the church, or God, or Nature.

But Nature is not Someone Else anymore. Nature—in our local region of the universe—has concentrated herself in our human energy, and what Nature does now to advance the evolution will be what *we* do. We *are* evolutionary Nature. Even God, we now realize, is not quite such an outsider, at least not to the point of taking our responsibilities for us. Teilhard several times told us, "God makes us make ourselves,"[4] but the weight of his word has not yet sunk deep into our minds.

Many of us continue to hope, in more or less hidden ways, that there will still be some special ones who will volunteer to carry the burden of anxiety and insecurity for us, who will do all this frightening thinking and planning and deciding, and we simple people can just go along with whatever "they" determine. But perhaps the deepest root of our very real fear of the future is that we can no longer look to the outside for authority. Maybe whatever authority there is, is within. Perhaps there is no "outside," as we had previously thought. If not, there must not be any outsiders. No "others" on whom to put the responsibility, no "They" to follow, no "Them" to blame. It may turn out that we are It in this game of evolving life, and that it is a matter of "all of us together." In Teilhard's words,

> The gates of the future are not thrown open to a few of the privi- leged nor to one chosen people to the exclusion of all others. They will open to an advance of *all together*, in a direction in which *all together* can join and find completion in a spiritual renovation of the earth.[5]

If we modify the popular spiritual in recognition of the interiority of Deity and our own responsibility, we may sing, "We've got all of us together in our hands: we've got the whole world in our hands."

The Whole World

If we are going to create the future, the first thing we must do, in Teilhard's view, is to cultivate a "sense of the Whole."[6] It is the sense of the whole that enables us to realize the truth about evolution. Without it, we are only playing with a theory, a certain way of ordering our ob- servations for specific conveniences. Evolution, as it functioned in Teilhard's consciousness, was "a *whole* which unfolds."[7] "Everything in the world appears and exists as a function of the whole," he asserts. "This is the broadest, deepest, and most unassailable meaning of the idea of evolution."[8]

For Teilhard, evolution is the gradual drawing together in a highly concentrated way of a multitude of ever more highly diversi- fied elements. We are familiar with this idea as Teilhard's principle of the creative and differentiating union.[9] The whole thus created bears the name *Omega,* the name both of the union finally achieved and of the immanent principle that had been at work throughout the process of unification from the very beginning.

> Omega appears to us fundamentally as the centre which is de- fined by the finite concentration upon itself of the noosphere— and indirectly, therefore, of all the isospheres that precede it. In

Omega, then, a maximum complexity, cosmic in extent, coincides with a maximum cosmic centricity.[10]

This is what Teilhard means by wholeness. It is the result of a progressive convergence of the varied materials of the universe around a unique center from which all the components derive their meaning, in terms of which they identify their differentiated functions, and through which they focus their energies.

This progressive convergence has come to the point where the next elements to be united are ourselves as reflexively conscious and free beings. Where is the unifying center located with respect to our human energies, which must be the subjects of its converging work? To unify our conscious energies, the center must itself be of the nature of consciousness: intelligible and lovable—and not an outside power imposing itself upon us, for free energies can never be unified by force. It must rather present itself to us as some single meaning and value that will magnetize all understandings and all affections.

We must become aware, says Teilhard, of the "unifying influence . . . of a destiny that is supremely attractive, the same for all at the same time." We must encourage "the general awakening of our consciousness to the vast and extreme organicity of the universe as a whole," so that we may experience "the emergence of a powerful field of internal attraction, in which we shall find ourselves caught *from within*."[11] We will not succeed in the further evolution of our consciousness without thus embracing and submitting ourselves to be embraced by the whole, for "ultimately, our thought cannot comprehend anything but the whole, nor, when it comes to the point, can our dreams entertain anything but the whole."[12]

It is my intention to extend and develop these themes of Teilhard's by suggesting that we need not only a consciousness of the whole, but a wholistic* consciousness. It is in terms of this wholistic consciousness that we may attain the projected convergence by acti-

*The spelling *wholistic*, rather than the more common *holistic*, is deliberately chosen here for the following reasons: The play on the words *whole* as entire, *whole* as healthy, *wholeness*, *wholesome*, *make whole*, *wholistic*, would be spoiled if the eye were not caught by the consistent spelling. Furthermore, the

vating another set of human energies than those most in evidence at the moment, and so create a desirable future.

The Grid of Partiality

Wholistic consciousness, of course, means the overcoming and absorbing of partial consciousness. Partial consciousness—which is only partially conscious—is consciousness of parts: the dividing consciousness that recognizes "this" as not being "that"—a very useful type of consciousness and one that should be used. But it has, in our recent past, the last few thousand years, all too often used us and been used against us. It has acted as a *consciousness of partiality*.

Having distinguished "this" from "that" with reference to some particular function or relative characteristic, the consciousness of partiality has proceeded to proclaim that "this" is better than "that" in itself, or absolutely, and is to be preferred to "that" on all occasions. Our culture has been formed as a patchwork of such partialities—the preference being given to the strong, the rich, the male sex, the white race, the industrialized nations—a crazy quilt of flashing satins held together by scraps of enduring burlap and despised gingham—not the wholeness of a seamless robe by any means.

We have believed in these partialities, in these divisions and preferences of the world. Everybody sustains them by their speech, their emotional response, and their behavior. The community's conviction has persuaded us that this is the way the world naturally is and ought to be. It is as though we had put a test-scoring template over the wholeness of our experience and then called only those exchanges between world-energies that happened to appear in the windows of the template "reality." What we call "the real world"—especially when we wish to reduce some wild-eyed idealist to the dust of ridicule— is only a pattern of partialities, a kind of *psychic grid* laid over the

---

word *holism* already has a history and rather special associations. I believe it will contribute to clarity and to better control over the images and ideas evoked by the word if we establish a fresh context and build up our own meaning within it.

wholeness of the universe to select those relations in terms of which we wish to organize our world.

A pattern of partialities is not a whole world, and its unwholesomeness is only too evident now, ranging all the way from personal hostilities, through economic and social injustices, ethnic and religious strife, class hatred, to international conflicts and global warfare. This unwholesomeness, I believe, derives very largely from the kind of psychic grid we have been using. I will call this grid, for convenience, the *grid of partiality*. Its paradigm is a collection of separate units subject to manipulation from without. When the units are organized, the organizing principle is *another* with respect to the organized; the governor is other than the governed. The organizer or governor is an outsider who exerts power over the organized and governed by will. The relation is arbitrary, not intrinsic. The resulting patterns can never be organic unions, for they are not unified from within to form integral wholes.

From this first assumption of separateness and division into parts, we can easily derive a long series of ills that characterize our contemporary culture: loneliness, alienation, rank gradation, class consciousness, discrimination, domination, exploitation, hostility, aggression, destruction. This sounds rather harsh, but consider: when the organizing and governing principle is ontologically separate from the organized and governed, the relations between them are necessarily contingent and unilateral. This means that insecurity attends the relationship from the outset, that there is tension among the relating parties, that hostility is always potential. Unilateral relationships tend to be power relationships, a contest to see whose will it is that will prevail. This leads to a rank ordering in terms of threat and obedience or conciliation, which can hardly escape being a temptation to class-discrimination, domination, and exploitation. If the dominated resist, the relationship deteriorates to force, punishment, aggression, and destruction.[13]

Peaceful relationships in this system must be uncontested domination relationships in which the lower orders do obey the higher. An entire community can be established in this way. It will then regard *other* communities in terms of the same pattern. It will attempt to dominate the other community and, to that end, will teach its members that they are better than the members of the other community and that they must have devotion to their own community as distinguished from all other communities. Various activities are developed in support, justification, and display of the superiority of the given community, and a certain amount of energy also goes into showing the inferiority of other communities. Racial discrimination is of this sort, as are the rivalries between different religious groups, or sexual stereotyping, or the kind of mentality that is encouraged when one country is engaged in hostilities (hot or cold) with another.

This is the psychic grid by which we are living today and which is activating our human energies. As U Thant has said, "The generation in power throughout the world . . . is still separatist and exclusivist in its thinking and in its policies."[14] Obviously, many people admire and approve this outlook on life. They feel that it is vigorous and hard. It is the way to advance; the best will come to the top. We were right, says William Safire, to "enhance our national pride at beating the Russians" in getting to the moon, and we should not have become "embarrassed at spending so much money on pure adventure when there were mouths to feed on earth." We need the challenge of danger, the emotional release and interest in life provided by adventure and competition, because "such contests and heroics provide the necessary moral equivalent of war."[15]

Elaine Morgan, tongue in cheek no doubt, suggests another equivalent. There may be reason to think now, she writes, that the huge stores of armaments being accumulated by the superpowers are functioning not so much as genuine weapon threats but rather as a display competition—as collectors' items![16]

In whatever form, it would seem that heroics are still our ideal. These behaviors are our version of two basic social phenomena common to primate communities. Individual heroics are practiced to gain dominance, or ascendancy in the rank-order, while group heroics form what is called the male bond, as in warfare against a common enemy.

What would happen to these basic social phenomena if we were to exercise our "sense of the whole" and really have a whole world? But this is just why we *cannot* have a whole world, according to Robert Heilbroner. National group bonding is a basic psychological tendency. The nation-state serves as a "valid surrogate for the family" and establishes "a powerful uniting bond," which has a fixed limitation causing its members to "look upon members of other states or groups with the same unseeing eye that the child fastens on someone who is merely an object and not a person."[17]

This leads to what Erik Erikson calls "pseudo-speciation," in which ethnic groups develop independently. The longer they continue in such separatist development, the more different they become. Konrad Lorenz, in *Civilized Man's Eight Deadly Sins*,[18] points out that "any clearly differentiated cultural group tends to consider itself a species apart . . . [and] does not accept the members of other, comparable units as of equal worth. In many native languages the term for one's own tribe is simply 'man'."[19]

Such considerations lead Heilbroner to conclude that it is "utopian to hope that we will face the global challenges of the future as an international brotherhood of men."[20] The fault, U Thant argues, lies not in some immutable human nature but in "the outdated attitudes, the narrow vision, the fears, suspicions, and selfishness of the [nation] states, and above all [in] their continued insistence on the primacy of unlimited national sovereignty."[21] An "outdated attitude," he says.

Is our custom, so entrenched as to be called "ineradicable instinct" by some observers, of dividing ourselves into competing groups no longer an advantageous character in terms of evolution? Konrad Lorenz declares that "competition between man and man works . . . as no biological factor has ever done before . . . in direct opposition to all the forces of nature, destroying nearly all the values these have created, with a cold calculation dictated exclusively by value-blind commercial considerations."[22]

That is precisely the trouble with the grid of partiality. It easily becomes the disastrous exaggeration of a fundamentally valuable mentality. In the instrumental and technical realm, the method of separation and identification by contrast is not only useful, it is indispensable. In our dealings with the material world and with the realms of abstraction we obviously benefit greatly from our skill in analysis and manipulation. But these methods can be carried too far—to universally destructive weapons, to poisonous by-products of desirable production, or to mechanistic compartmentalization of people to fit statistical classes and bureaucratic schedules. When we try to do everything by reduction to categories and external control, we lose our sense of the whole and our awareness that this is basically a *personalizing universe*.[23]

We lose our feelings for other creatures and see them as mere objects in the world. Heilbroner mentions the importance our culture sets on the value of "efficiency, with its tendency to subordinate the optimum human scale of things to the optimum technical scale," the "value of the need to 'tame' the environment, with its consequence of an unthinking pillage of nature," the "value of the priority of production itself," resulting in "indifference to the aesthetic aspects of life."[24] And Lorenz remarks sadly that we no longer have the ability to feel awe, because we are so alienated from nature: our "utilitarian way of thinking . . . turns the means into the end and forgets the original aim."[25]

Some of the wisest and most beautiful statements on this problem that I have seen are made by Joan McIntyre in her extraordinary book, *Mind in the Waters*. As things are now, she comments, "we are bound to a vision that leads us further away from nature, and further away from each other. It is our loneliness as much as our greed which can destroy us." The consequence of this, if we do not find another way of looking at things, she warns, will be "the death of the planet, and the death of the spirit of the planet." We have analyzed and manipulated ourselves almost to extinction. We need to join experience and thought—to experience the world mentally as a whole. We need to "take a second look." And when we do, we should remember that "the truth . . . can be more easily found by people viewing a whole world."[26]

Wholistic Consciousness

What I want to suggest now is that the worldview of partiality, this habit of dividing ourselves into separate groups and cultivating a consciousness of fear, hostility, suspicion, and selfishness, is not an ineradicable instinct, but only a psychic grid; that we are not helpless and passive in its clutches, but free to create alternative states of consciousness in which our human energies may be activated in quite different patterns.

As already proposed, the psychic grid is like a template placed over an examination paper that permits only those answers that we deem correct to show through. Another image for this grid—and the one for which it was originally named[27]—is drawn from the triode form of the electron tube, which consists of a cathode emitting electrons, an anode receiving them, and a "grid" between them that can amplify, diminish, or otherwise pattern the stream of electrons that pass it to be received by the anode.

We know that everything that goes on in this universe involves some sort of energy exchange. Here, in the midst of evolution, there are an enormous number of energy and information exchanges going on. It is these exchanges that we receive whenever we experience anything and that we initiate or engage in whenever we do anything. We can call them "intercommunications," and since the universe as we are presently living in it consists of these intercommunications, we can call it an *intercommunicating universe*.[28]

In making this model of the psychic grid, I liken the intercommunicating universe to the cathode, and I suppose it to consist of an indefinite infinity of intercommunications. The anode represents our reflexive consciousness, that is, our consciousness as we experience being conscious. The grid between is the system of organizing and interpreting the world that we use, the pattern of perceptions and powers that we regard as defining "reality." The model then suggests that what the grid does is shut out some of the emissions coming from the cathode, allowing only certain ones to get through to the anode. That is, we are conscious only of a selection of intercommunications, ordered in a pattern that is imposed by the grid.

The point I wish to make is that there is a grid in operation in our consciousness. The world that fills our consciousness, in which we perceive certain things and do certain things, is not congruent with the intercommunicating universe itself. It is not unreal, but it is only one possible way of patterning reality. There are other ways, and we are able to choose among them to some extent. We have a "feedback loop" to the grid.

In order to avoid misunderstanding, let me say here that in proposing a "wholistic" grid instead of our present grid of partiality, I hold that the former is still a grid. Even if we view the world in a more "wholistic" way, we will still not be receiving all the intercommunications from the indefinitely infinite universe. The wholistic grid is only another way of patterning reality, one which, I will argue, has certain advantages over our present way of doing things, but it is not the ultimate answer or the absolute view of reality.

There are five attributes, I think, that characterize the grid of wholistic consciousness: (1) simultaneity of perception, (2) coincidence of sameness and difference, (3) organization by an immanent principle, (4) reverence for each and for the All, and (5) motivation arising from the Whole.

The wholistic consciousness perceives the world as fundamentally one, that is, it grasps it all at once as if it were a single being, takes it all in at one glance, rather than lining it up item-wise, piecemeal. In this respect wholistic consciousness is more like our faculty of vision than our faculty of hearing. Hearing, for us, is sequential, one sound after another. It is related to our sense of time; it is linear. Seeing, on the other hand, is simultaneous, a number of items are perceived at once, but all as composing one scene. It gives us our clearest sense of space; it is three-dimensional.

The grid of partiality sees things first as separate, then as put together. The grid of wholeness sees things first as together, then as distinct within this togetherness. The linear image for partiality represents its narrowness of perspective and its tendency to deal with all situations in terms of a pair of opposites. (The only internal distinctions that can be made in a line are compounds of bifurcation.) A wholistic consciousness is multidimensional: many types of interrelations are possible within it. There can be more variables, and their relations can be more complex.

This is closely related to the second quality, the coincidence of sameness and difference, or unity and multiplicity. Wholistic consciousness sees the entire scene at once, as one vista; everything in the perceived space is grasped simultaneously. It also sees each item in the space in its distinction from every other item. It sees the manyness of all the elements, sees each in its own unique individuality.

And it sees the oneness of the single being that all of them together compose. This is what constitutes "wholeness." Wholeness is not the same as simple unity. It is unity *and* multiplicity simultaneously grasped and equally valued.

Wholeness is not a unity of homogeneity but a unity that is expressed by the interactions of the component members. It is a unity of operation, of process, even of purpose. All the elements constitute one being because they are all *doing* one thing. And it takes all of them to do it. Therefore their *heterogeneity* is essential to the unity. Each element has a unique role; but that role makes sense only within the whole. Thus the oneness and the manyness of a whole imply one another and depend on one another for their being and their meaning. The unity, sameness, difference, and multiplicity all characterize the same entity simultaneously and by mutual implication.

It is evident how this differs from the grid of partiality. There the heterogeneity is *between* the groups, and *within* the groups there is homogeneity—with respect to whatever principle of grouping is being used. The homogeneous group is seen as one, over against another homogeneous group. The sameness is in one place (within the group), and the difference in another (between the groups). In the grid of wholeness, the sameness and difference are in the same place, actually meaning the same thing in different ways, that is, they both mean wholeness. In the grid of partiality any element or any one homogeneous group is identified by its difference, that is, its opposition to another element or group. It is what it is by not being the other. There is mutual rejection and exclusion between the groups—at least logically, if in no other way. But when there is logical rejection—for instance, the definition of being "Protestant" excludes or rejects the possibility of being "Catholic" and vice versa—it is disastrously easy to pass to class rejection and even to warfare, as we have witnessed in Northern Ireland.

The grid of wholeness, however, would not begin by perceiving people in these terms. The ordering principle in wholeness is not one that classifies items by their differences but one that identifies each element in terms of its cooperation with all the others within the one overarching unity to which there can be no opposite.

In that case, the unity must come from within; the governing principle must be immanent to the governed, not imposed from without. This unity is not achieved by domination. The governing principle must act as a center for focusing the energy exchanges of all the individuals. It must be a center of centers, as Teilhard so well said.[29]

If one great principle is acting as central focus for all the inter-communicating energies of the wholistic community, then no part can claim privileges over any other part, or assert that that part exists only to be of service to the first. Partialistic domination within the whole is impossible. Each element and each local organization of elements is primarily an end in itself, related essentially to the great central principle and, through it and in terms of it, to all the other parts.

This means that every part of the universe is worthy of reverence and no part may be exploited. Even nonhuman beings have rights of their own; their meaning is not exhausted by a description of how we can use or enjoy them. Those of us who are free beings and do manipulate other parts of the universe, therefore, have a serious obligation to try to discern the pattern being developed by the spirit of the whole and to follow it. We have no right to set ourselves apart and appropriate the rest of the universe—or as much of it as we can get our hands on—without any consideration of what the overall function of the world is or of what the individual rights of the parts within it may be. Both of these values have to be held in balance.

If we are not to see other items in the universe in terms of their usefulness or pleasure for ourselves, if we cannot refer everything else to our benefit in order to establish its value, if we are not to strive to improve our situation by so ordering the rest of the world with respect to our advancement, what kinds of action shall we take and what can possibly motivate us? Are we not to be stimulated by competition and enticed by the prospect of personal profit? After all, the spice of life comes from opposition and challenge; pleasure comes from winning, and satisfaction comes from gain that is personally experienced. Who will confess to an interest in working for "the Whole"?

Such questions make us realize that the grid is not only a framework for perceiving and interpreting, but also for valuing, feeling, and behaving. Having been reared in our particular culture, we may sincerely feel that it is quite impossible to motivate anyone to exert themselves for any reason other than one's own gain in some sense. In other words, the reference has to come back for its ultimate stability and justification to the individual standing apart and separate from every other individual. That is the grid of partiality as we experience it in our feelings.

But the grid of wholistic consciousness can also frame feelings that are commensurate with its visions and judgments. The ultimate value in this view is the Whole itself, that is, the entire world, each individual in it, and the immanent central principle. What motivates any individual within the Whole, then, is the desire that the Whole should continue to progress on its path of becoming a more perfect Whole—that is, continue to attain greater complexity and greater unity. But since the "wholeness" of the Whole depends on the uniqueness and cherished value of all its composing individuals, any individual within the Whole will also be moved to respond to each other individual in terms of his or her unique individuality—for this value also must be protected. It cannot be oppressed or neglected on the excuse that we are looking to the welfare of the Whole.

Again, these two motives have to be held in balance, but both are equally to be distinguished from motives arising from partiality, the favoring of one part of the Whole at the expense of others. Moreover, this emotional outlook will have very beneficial consequences for the individuals who practice it, for it will relieve them of the very stresses that we enumerated as characterizing the grid of partiality: loneliness, alienation, hostility, fear, suspicion, envy, and many other detrimental psychic energy formations that are presently draining our strength. All of the human energies so liberated would, under the grid of wholeness, be available for improving the lot of all creatures who must live together here.

The Conviction Community

If this grid of wholistic consciousness has so many advantages over the grid of partiality, why are we not using it? The culture in general is not using it because we have been initiated into membership in a conviction community, which perceives the world through the grid of partiality.

The establishment of a grid is always a community affair. *Human consciousness is essentially a shared consciousness.* If the universe is composed of an indefinite infinity of intercommunicating energies, the psychic grids are formed by communities of human energies inter-communicating in terms of common "conviction spaces." No one can have human consciousness without sharing in some conviction space, without membership in some conviction community. The very complexity of our psychic energy exchanges—especially through language and other forms of symbolization—is what constitutes the overwhelming unity of our noospheric community and gives our consciousness its reflexivity, clarity, subtlety, and precision. The shared conviction system is the necessary foundation for this development of differentiation.

I use *conviction* here to include concepts, attitudes, values, beliefs, whatever belongs to the general worldview that we are consciously and unconsciously assuming. The unconscious convictions, of course, are even more important than the conscious ones, for we are so convinced of them that we simply take them for granted as "reality" and proceed to perceive the rest of the world in terms of them. A *conviction space* is the world of perceptions and behaviors structured by the conviction system, or psychic grid, of a given community and uncritically regarded by it as the real world.

As don Juan explained to Carlos Castaneda, "the real world" is a "description" that we have learned from the consensus of the community in which we were reared. When we are infants, he said, the world is described to us by adults (by words, emotional attitudes, body language, behavior—both things done and things not done) until we become capable of actually perceiving it according to that description.[30] Then we become members of the community that shares this particular description, that lives in this particular conviction space.

The conviction space thus defines for the community the limits of reality, possibility, and desirability. It pronounces on the natures of things. Indeed, since all the consciously received perceptions, all the spoken concepts, and all the orderly behavior in the community are themselves structured in terms of the conviction space, it seems to the members of the community that they are objectively justified in viewing the world as they do. Each one's experience confirms a neighbor's, convincing all that they are perceiving the world as it really is.

Conviction systems do not, of course, just spring up like mushrooms and impose themselves arbitrarily upon unsuspecting communities. As Marvin Harris has shown in his scholarly and entertaining book, *Cows, Pigs, Wars, and Witches: The Riddles of Culture*,[31] even the most bizarre and seemingly irrational and nonfunctional customs and beliefs are rooted in adaptation schemes that favor the survival of the community in its habitat. However, they frequently continue to mold the minds and behavior of the members long after that particular adaptation scheme has become obsolete.

The other side of this situation is revealed in an article on "Language and Reality" by George B. Leonard,[32] who remarks on how our experience is effectively limited by our language. Language is formulated within some particular conviction system, but once formulated, it operates as a positive feedback, reinforcing the system. Leonard points out that if there are no adequate words for a possible human experience in a given culture, that experience will stand outside the limits of the real for most people in that culture. A culture, he claims, by depriving its individuals of a vocabulary for a certain type of experience is exercising the most effective censorship possible over this type of experience.

In either case, for useful adaptation or for limitation of experience, this is how psychic grids are established and how they are maintained. How are they changed? Here, what Thomas Kuhn has to say in *The Structure of Scientific Revolutions*[33] is quite relevant. Science operates, he tells us, by paradigms—ways of defining and seeing the scientific world, ways of structuring scientific questions and of proceeding to answer those questions. As long as a particular paradigm is working, normal scientific activity goes forward. Eventually observations begin to appear that do not fit the paradigm. At first, these are ignored or rejected, but as the anomalies accumulate, there comes a time when the paradigm itself is questioned, and a period of uncertainty and insecurity ensues.

New paradigms are introduced that compete with one another. It is important to notice that, contrary to our naive assumption, there is no neutral ground of "pure" observation and "impartial" conceptualization where any given paradigm may be judged as "true" or "false." But in terms of what constitutes scientific *life* in that period of history, one paradigm will eventually emerge as more *viable* than the others. At first, only a few people—often young or new to the field whose imaginations are not so firmly fixed in the previous paradigm—who are drawn, perhaps as much by the new theory's "neatness" and "simplicity" as by its ability to solve problems, improve measurements, and predict novel phenomena, will adopt a proposed paradigm and work with it. By doing so, they manifest to their colleagues what it would be like to belong to a community guided by this grid, and they thus gain a few more converts. These also expand and multiply the persuasive arguments, as well as the technology and literature relative to the new form. This demonstration of actual scientific life in terms of the new view draws in great numbers of practicing scientists, until gradually the new paradigm has become the fundamental worldview for the vast majority of the community and the basis for normal scientific activity.

It is interesting to observe that a somewhat similar phenomenon occurs in art and in fashion, that is, in our perception of aesthetic values, as distinguished from our attempts to find a theoretical and intellectual organization for the world. A famous fashion designer once pointed out that whenever a new fashion appears, it is at first perceived as ugly. But the designer arranges for beautiful people to wear the new fashion, and this association gradually encourages local social leaders to adopt the new style. As its use spreads, the perception of it changes. The eye adjusts to it and after a while sees it as beautiful and right. This endures for a time, usually until a noticeably different style is introduced. Then, as the new one gains ground, the old one is perceived as dowdy.

This is how grids are changed in the community. I think we should underscore a common element in these different examples: a small group first demonstrates what it would be like in practical fact to live under the new grid. Teilhard himself admitted, in a footnote to the passage in which he declared that the future will open only to all of us together, that this may have to come about under the influence of a few, an elite.[34]

In our case, we may say that Teilhard has proposed to us a new psychic grid, the sense of the Whole, and if we will act as the trend-setters, as the beautiful people, the young, the imaginative, the open-minded ones who dare to adopt the new grid and to live by it, demonstrating what it would be like to belong to a community guided by this paradigm, then perhaps it will begin to spread and to become the general consciousness of our culture.

The Convergence Perspective

Teilhard said that we are evolution and that we have the responsibility for continuing our advance by creating our own future. The apparent line of advance is toward more complexity, more consciousness, more freedom, more interiority, more recognition of the central immanent principle that is simultaneously unifying and differentiating the elements that compose its wholeness. We seem to have strayed from this line by falling under the spell of the psychic grid of partiality, which has prevented us from perceiving the world as whole. This has resulted in various ills from which we are presently suffering.

If we now ask, what can we do to heal our world, to *make it whole*, one answer may be, let us try to acquire the psychic grid of wholistic consciousness and to incorporate into it the grid of part-by-part analysis, restricting the latter to those specific functions for which it is truly useful. This effort should include the scientific investigation of why certain grids characterize our communities, what their relations are to the ecological and economic facts of life, and what modifications of them can be made by moral means.

I repeat that the community must live together in some kind of shared consciousness and common conviction system. We cannot each go off in a private dreamworld of our own. And it is not a matter of concocting just any novel view of the world. If we undertake to improve our psychic grid, the new version must be a practical, livable view, one that promotes community life in greater complexity/consciousness and higher-level personhood, a harmonious exchange of human energies. If we now understand that there is a grid in operation in our consciousness, we shall be better prepared to apply our intelligence to it, to trace out its roots, and to seek adaptations that represent genuine advances in evolution.

Because any psychic grid is a shared consciousness, and the establishment and alteration of grids is a community enterprise, no one is excused from this work. We must all strive to acquire the wholistic mode of perception and to encourage it by word and behavior in our neighbors. Again, because the wholistic consciousness is also a consciousness of the Whole, no one can be left out. No one is to be considered as "other" or regarded as an "outsider." This principle must govern also the attitude of the advocate of wholistic consciousness toward adherents to the grid of partiality. The we/they consciousness is to be progressively forsaken in favor of the "ever greater We."[35]

This is only a way of saying that we must so activate our human energies as to promote their *convergence*. Whatever we perceive, whatever we imagine, think, or judge, whatever we feel or value, is an expression of human energy. All our external actions, our behaviors, are outgrowths of these psychic energies.[36] Therefore, we should first concentrate our efforts on shifting the pattern of our psychic energies into modalities of convergence, activating another set of human energies.

The grid of partiality has encouraged us to value distinction, opposition, competition, hostility, success. We have attempted to gain knowledge by taking things apart. In morals and religion we have been presented with either/or choices. In law we use the adversary model. Interest and significance are generated by the conflict/resolution pattern in storytelling, including history, even sacred history. All of these are activations of human energy in *divergent* modes.

A certain amount of this was good and necessary at an earlier stage of our evolution. In certain situations it is still appropriate. My suggestion, however, is that we are now passing over the equator, to use Teilhard's familiar image,[37] and the meridians of our energies that have been expressed in divergence should now begin to be expressed in convergence.

Perceived through the grid of wholistic consciousness, the world would appear as a pattern of inter-independence, complementarity, cooperation, friendship, and creative joy. Knowledge would be drawn from the level on which elements are synthesized, intelligibility being recognized as located in the Whole. In human relations and the moral and religious insights that guide them, we would work by "both/and" methods, rather than "either/or," striving for inclusion of all and reconciliation of differences. We would find our delight in giving ourselves freely and totally to the creative processive Whole, in company with all who together compose it and are themselves creatively contributing to it, each in a unique way.[38]

We will then evolve, freely and creatively, by sharing our conscious energies more deeply, more intimately, and more intensely. This will cause us to draw closer to, and to center ourselves more profoundly on, the immanent principle that unifies the Whole. This in turn will promote the differentiation of each individual member of the Whole. The more conscious the individual becomes, the more the individual becomes *person*; and person is person only to the extent that the individual freely lives by the life of the Whole. So the more the individuals are differentiated, the more the persons will exchange their human energies in the great complex of the Whole and draw closer and closer together in freely willed personal union. The evolution of personal consciousness becomes thus a spiral of convergence, activated by delight in creating the future.

The future is the evolution of conscious energies, and the evolution of conscious energies is achieved by our own free creation of the Whole, which ever looks toward the future. As Teilhard saw in his prophetic vision, "Nothing holds together absolutely except through the Whole, and the Whole itself holds together only through its future fulfillment."[39]

Notes

1. Pierre Teilhard de Chardin, *The Phenomenon of Man* (New York: Harper, 1959), p. 231.

2. Teilhard, *The Appearance of Man* (New York: Harper & Row, 1956), p. 224; *The Vision of the Past* (New York: Harper & Row, 1966), p. 262.

3. Walter Kaufmann, *Without Guilt and Justice: From Decidophobia to Autonomy* (New York: Wyden, 1973).

4. Teilhard, *The Vision of the Past*, pp. 25, 154; *Christianity and Evolution* (New York: Harcourt Brace Jovanovich, 1971), p. 28.

5. Teilhard, *The Phenomenon of Man*, p. 244.

6. Teilhard, *Christianity and Evolution*, p. 102 (cf. pp. 57 ff.); *Science and Christ* (New York: Harper & Row, 1968), pp. 43, 56; *The Future of Man* (New York: Harper & Row, 1964), p. 17; *Human Energy* (New York: Harcourt Brace Jovanovich, 1969), p. 82.

7. Teilhard, *The Phenomenon of Man*, p. 35.

8. Teilhard, *The Future of Man*, p. 214.

9. Teilhard, *The Phenomenon of Man*, pp. 31, 262. Cf. Beatrice Bruteau, *Evolution Toward Divinity* (Wheaton, IL: Theosophical Publishing House, 1974), pp. 82–83.

10. Teilhard, *Activation of Energy* (New York: Harcourt Brace Jovanovich, 1971), p. 111.

11. Teilhard, *The Future of Man*, pp. 285, 287.

12. Teilhard, *Christianity and Evolution*, pp. 57–58.

13. For a development of this line of analysis as applied to patriarchal theology and its alternatives, see Bruteau, "The Image of the Virgin-Mother," in *Women and Religion*, ed. J. Plaskow and J. A. Romero (Missoula, Montana: The Scholars Press, 1974).

14. U Thant, "Reflections of a Mediator," *World* 7/4/72, p. 39.

15. William Safire, *New York Times* News Service (December 1974).

16. Elaine Morgan, *The Descent of Woman* (New York: Stein & Day, 1972), p. 190.

17. Robert L. Heilbroner, *An Inquiry into the Human Prospect* (New York: Norton, 1974), pp. 112–113. See also the interview with Heilbroner by Coline Campbell, "Coming Apart at the Seams," *Psychology Today* (February 1975); esp. p. 100: "Campbell: Do you admire the kind of nation-state you're talking about? Doesn't nationalism *usually* lead to war?—Heilbroner: I loathe the nation-state. . . . But it's the only political community we have these days. . . . The damned thing is necessary. . . . Maybe in 75 years we'll have achieved a viable social system. Perhaps the terrible division between rich and poor will have ended . . . more humane community . . . more religious . . . more artistic, more erotic, more penurious, more political . . . people talking about what they should do and how. . . . If there's a prototype toward which our society is moving, it would be the monastery . . . a sense of social purpose, of shared aims . . . everyone . . . conscious of being part of a larger organization."

18. Konrad Lorenz, *Civilized Man's Eight Deadly Sins*, trans. M. K. Wilson (New York: Harcourt Brace Jovanovich, 1974), p. 65.

19. In our own language, the male "tribe" calls itself, as well as the species, "man."

20. Heilbroner, p. 113.

21. U Thant, loc. cit.

22. Lorenz, p. 26.

23. Cf. Teilhard, *The Phenomenon of Man*, pp. 260, 290; also, "Sketch of a Personalistic Universe," in *Human Energy*, pp. 53–89. See also Beverly Wildung Harrison, "The New Consciousness of Women: A Socio-Political Resource," *Cross Currents* XXIV (1975), pp. 445–462, on the crisis provoked by the exclusion of lived-world interpersonal values from the public sector of our lives and their relegation to the private world known as "woman's place."

24. Heilbroner, p. 77.

25. Lorenz, p. 98.

26. Joan McIntyre, *Mind in the Waters: A Book to Celebrate the Consciousness of Whales and Dolphins* (New York: Scribner's, 1974), pp. 8, 9, 95.

27. These ideas, first expressed in a lecture in 1971, were later developed by the author in *The Psychic Grid: How We Create the World We Know* (Wheaton, Ill.: Quest, 1979), p. 49.

28. Ibid., pp. 152ff.

29. Teilhard, *The Phenomenon of Man*, p. 271; *Christianity and Evolution*, p. 137.

30. Carlos Castaneda, *Journey to Ixtlan* (New York: Simon and Schuster, 1972), pp. 8–9; cf. *A Separate Reality* (New York: Simon and Schuster, 1971), p. 302.

31. Marvin Harris, *Cows, Pigs, Wars, and Witches: The Riddles of Culture* (New York: Random House, 1974).

32. George B. Leonard, "Language and Reality," *Harper's* (November 1974).

33. Thomas S. Kuhn, *The Structure of Scientific Revolutions*, 2d ed. (Univ. of Chicago Press, 1970).

34. Teilhard, *The Phenomenon of Man*, p. 244.

35. Cf. Teilhard's "ever greater Christ," *Letters from a Traveller* (New York: Harper & Row, 1962), pp. 133, 305.

36. Cf. Teilhard, *The Phenomenon of Man*, p. 64: "All energy is psychical in nature."

37. Ibid., p. 242.

38. Cf. Bruteau, "The Image of the Virgin-Mother"; also "The Divine Mother and the Convergence of the World," *World Union* Souvenir Volume (December 1973).

39. Teilhard, *Christianity and Evolution*, p. 71.

SEVEN

Global Spirituality and the Integration of East and West

As astronomer Fred Hoyle predicted in 1948, "Once a photograph of the earth, taken from outside, is available—once the sheer isolation of the earth becomes plain, a new idea as powerful as any in history will be let loose."[1] This powerful idea is that we human beings—better, perhaps, we living beings—constitute one family on a tiny fragile planet in limitless space.

For millions of years, we Earth-people have identified and valued ourselves by contrasting our immediate tribe with the tribe next door. The background for having a sense of who *we* are has been "other people." "Other people" were the ground and "we" were the figure. We—whoever we were—were the norm of human being, and others were outsiders, aliens, barbarians, savages, gentiles, pagans, infidels. But when we see Earth from deep space, we know that the only ground against which we can be seen is the emptiness of the abyss.

A fundamental method of organizing our experience has been undermined. The contrast method, by which we perceive figure against ground, sound against silence; by which we conceive one idea in distinction from all others that it is not; by which we value one object above another, one act above another, one person above

another—this fundamental method has been shaken because its paradigm, the sense of who *we* are in our tribe as against *them* in their
tribe, has been shown to be utterly incommensurate with the reality
of our situation.

How shall we say who we are, now that we know we are all one?
Since we need a new method of thinking and feeling about ourselves,
we also need a new global spirituality for the future. A popular way of
putting this has been to speak of an integration of East and West, but
even this is now obsolete. What is required is a unitary view that is
original and drawn from our experience itself, not something patched
together from the materials of the past.

This is not to say that we may overlook the fact that we are de-
scendants from that past and that its genes have shaped our present
lives. Indeed, we inherit all the traditions of all the cultures of this
planet. None of us is limited to the heredity of one tribe alone. Today,
however, as the incumbents of the present age, we must bring to birth
a vision of reality in which the features of this global inheritance will
be plainly visible, but whose unity, vitality, and thrust toward the future will be its own.

Children of God

"You are gods, children of the Most High, all of you." —Ps. 82:6

"Beloved, we are God's children." —1 John 3:2

That we are all children of God is a familiar idea, but it has never
been taken seriously and literally enough. Most traditions have used this
notion, or something equivalent, to tell us who we are, that we are ultimately descended from the Supreme Being and therefore have dignity and value. It has also served to set the in-group apart from the
out-group. In reaction, it has been deliberately employed by some
individuals—Jesus and Gandhi come immediately to mind—to reject
the division of their societies into castes and classes of relative honor.

Gandhi called those whom others regarded as "untouchable"
Harijan, children of Hari, God who has stolen our hearts. This was

not the first time such a teaching had been presented to the Indian people, for the Buddha had broken definitively with the caste system some twenty-five centuries earlier. That the same point had to be made again so much later only shows how reluctant we are to give up classifying and comparing ourselves with one another and preferring some classes to others.

Jesus, too, had said plainly that no one was to be given a privileged title of honor, because "You are all brothers," and he had taken pains to point out the authoritarian style of the Gentiles and to warn his companions not to imitate it.[2] Nevertheless, the institutions we have erected ostensibly in his honor are structured hierarchically and ruled by distinct classes of persons distinguished by their respective titles, costumes, and powers over those beneath them. That all people are equal because equally children of God is not a popular doctrine when it comes to practice. It is one of those hard sayings—who can bear to hear it?

What does it really mean, and how can it open to us a new method for understanding ourselves and relating to our world? Suppose we put ourselves in Jesus' place and try to imagine the experience he had in connection with his baptism. We may assume that his meditations on the meaning of life—his own and that of Israel—had been leading up to this moment. What, after all, are human beings? What—who—is any one of us, we who are intense points of personal awareness in the midst of a world of meaningless suffering, where God is mostly silent? Who am I? we constantly cry into the void. Let me purify myself, we say, let me wash away all that is not my truest self, let me dissolve all that is not the inmost core of my existence. Let me be baptized in this renunciation that I may see my central reality and know my true name.

Thus Jesus comes to John and is baptized by him. And as he came up out of the water, it seemed to him that the heavens opened to him and the Spirit of God descended upon him as if it were a dove; and he heard a voice say to him, "You are my beloved son in whom I am well pleased."[3]

Jesus did not receive this word that he was a child of God as a cliché, but as the stunning revelation it was meant to be. Over-whelmed by this realization, he was driven by the Spirit into the wilderness, where he remained fasting and praying for forty days. "If you are the child of God, then . . . ?" How many answers to this question did Jesus try? We know at least that he immediately rejected a number of possibilities. Being a child of God does not mean that you are to use magic to fulfill your material desires. It does not mean that you are to defy the laws of nature and expect miracles to sustain you. It does not mean that you are to dominate the rest of the world.

He also evidently came to some positive conclusions that show in his later preaching and behavior. Being a child of God does mean that you are to regard all as equal, to be as impartial as God, who sends sun and rain on just and unjust alike. It does mean that you are to love your enemies as well as your friends. You are to deepen your purity beyond ritual observance. You are to rejoice and consider your-self blessed even in circumstances that the judgment of the world ac-counts as misfortune.

In this view, those whom our caste-consciousness has deemed last come out first—first in the sense that everyone is first, for all are rewarded alike by the divine generosity. The comparative measures that we have been accustomed to use have been discarded. All are equally worthy, and equally unworthy, for worthiness is not the issue. To be a child of God means that your real life is maintained by God and is not measured by your manipulation of the environment. It means that you forgive and heal your sisters and brothers endlessly, as God endlessly forgives and heals you, continuing to pour life into you from moment to moment. It means that you live your true life in each other person, as each of them lives in you. It means that you give your life to be the nourishment of all and hold nothing back for your-self alone. It means that you are a sacrifice for the people and that the more you give yourself up in this way, the more you will rise to new-ness of life and ascend into divine union.

This is a tremendous answer. In many ways it is familiar, but it is also unexplored or unassimilated: for we still do not practice it. Why? Part of the reason may be that we retain a metaphysical view that contradicts it. The vision of reality that Jesus has outlined is incom-patible with our routine assumption that we are all separate, isolated, but comparable units.

In order to practice the politics of the children of God, we need to understand, and be converted to, the metaphysics that underlies these moral propositions. This is where our united heritage from East and West begins to be functional. Affirming both the nondualism that has been the central insight of the East and the personal freedom that has been the chief value of the West, we can gain an overall picture of our reality, a picture that would constitute a new method of ordering and appreciating our experience.

Let me be clear: I take the image "children of God" literally— that is, children truly inherit the nature of the parent. If God is represented as having a certain character, God's parenthood implies that his children also have it. Thus, if God is holy, his children are to be seen as holy. If God is indefinable, that is our clue that each human person is also indefinable.

What does it mean to be children of God in the light of a metaphysics of global spirituality? In summary, I would say that it means to be incomparable, to be love, to be *perichoresis*, and to be incarnate as creative process.

To Be Children of God Is to Be Incomparable

"To whom will you compare me?" —Isa. 46:5

"When they measure themselves by one another, and compare themselves with one another, they are without understanding." —2 Cor. 10:12

Here is the basic notion of this metaphysics, without which the rest of the system will not work. The real person is incomparable, incommensurable, indefinable, indescribable, not to be known or valued by reference to or relation to something else. In this sense the children of God can be said to be absolute and transcendent like their Parent. There is fear of this doctrine in some quarters on the grounds that it threatens the transcendence of God, as though in order for God to be properly transcendent there must be other beings from whom God can be distinguished and to whom God is utterly superior.

But transcendence really means that the transcendent being is simply free of any necessary reference to whatever it transcends. It is precisely its not being compared with those beings that makes it transcend them.

A sense for our own absolute, or nonrelative, being is the key to the freedom that will enable us to see ourselves in a new way, as if from outer space, and to form a deeply unitive community for the whole Earth. There first has to come a moment of what looks like complete withdrawal of each being from each other, because each is said to be independent of any comparison with others. Ordinarily, we recognize our physical, intellectual, and emotional dependence on one another and believe that recognition and affirmation of our interdependence is the foundation of the ideal community. But interdependence, a sharing and dovetailing of lacks, is not the ideal. Perhaps we might call the ideal community "inter-independent," for it must be a more intimate sharing of life than can be achieved by merely filling up each other's deficiencies. We are looking for a unity based not on deficiency but on superabundance.

Let us consider what happens when we define ourselves by dependence, relation, and comparison. Don't we superficially answer the great baptismal question—"What name shall we give?" "Who are you?"—by citing our occupation, our relation to spouse or parent or child, our nationality, our religion, our race, our wealth, our fame, our achievements, or perhaps some special feature that looms large in our social life such as sexual orientation, or some physical or mental handicap, or a drug dependency, or a prison record? Don't many of us build our lives around this particular descriptive answer? This is often how we think of ourselves and of other people. Our self-esteem and sense of having a satisfactory life are framed in these terms. We struggle and strain to be able to say to ourselves and others, my description is valued in my society. Or, if we cannot do that, we try to get our description valued as highly as one we have been denied: we declare that being the way *we* are is just as good and beautiful as the way *they* are. But we still think that we *are* this description. And our life consists of trying to get the description valued, or trying to get the valued description. It doesn't occur to us that our value doesn't lie in the description at all.

Notice that when we define ourselves by descriptions and comparisons and relations the value comes from scarcity. As long as I have the only Lincoln Continental on my block, I'm an important person. As soon as every garage on the street has a Continental in it, mine doesn't count any more. The comparison, the contrast, insured the value and gave me a sense of who I am. Much the same is true of our sense of achievement. If everyone can run the four-minute mile, I have no sense of accomplishment in doing it. This seems so right to us that we even say, "Where all are honored, no one is honored."

Our notion of value seems to be that in order for anything to be valuable, it has to be scarce. Because some people—most people— don't have it, we believe it's good. Deprivation, nonbeing, is the foundation of this sense of value.

Our feeling good about ourselves thus depends on other people's feeling bad. They must wish that they could have what we have, or do what we do, in order for our possession or our achievement to be important. If no one else wanted to have it, then even if I were the only one in the world to have it, my Lincoln would be worthless. Comparison, contrast—someone up, someone down—that is the way our judgment of life goes.

Even in a casual encounter some shadow of this standard governs our interchange. Can my personality dominate the other? Can I succeed in getting my opinion accepted, my choice deferred to? Can I get my way? Can I have the last word? Even in subtle ways this criterion operates: Didn't I handle that situation better than he did? Wasn't I more virtuous, more charitable, more humble? Whatever it is that we value, we convince ourselves that we have it by comparing ourselves with our neighbors.

What happens when we are not top dog? When we are deprived, poor, oppressed, rejected, despised, ridiculed, ignored? We are hurt, not only in our physical poverty or cultural deprivation, but in our sense of ourselves. My "Who I Am" is injured, and this injury seeks compensation. Because the sense of value is a contrast sense, this injury can be compensated *either* by attaining the value of which we were deprived, *or* by putting some others down, so that in comparison with them we now are on top. Then those underdogs will in turn have to do the same thing in compensation for their injury, and a chain of sin will be forged, and the hurts of one generation of inter-acting persons or races or classes or nations are passed on to manacle succeeding generations.

All this doesn't come about simply because people are evil or greedy or weak or proud. It comes about because of the way we have structured our sense of value, making it depend on comparison, depri-vation, frustration, injury. This in turn is related to our assumption that we *are* our descriptions, our relations to persons and institutions, our possession of a set of definable attributes.

It is important to understand this if we want to serve peace and justice, to lift up the poor and free the oppressed. We can then under-stand that fighting, defeating, depriving, and oppressing are *systematic necessities of our present mentality*. We have to have the contrast in order to have the sense of value, in order to have the sense of Who We Are.

Our present structures are full of injustice, but we cannot accom-plish our purpose simply by placing the currently oppressed class over those who now have goods and power. The contrast would break out again somewhere else. What we need to change is the deeply in-grained mentality that requires contrast in order to feel real and feel good. This can be done—if we understand how our real self tran-scends our descriptions.

The quest for the real self has perhaps more preoccupied the East than the West. Sage after sage has meditated on human suffering and asked, "Who am I?" Again and again the answer has come back: Suf-fering is involved in everything about our lives as we presently live them. It is caused by our craving for the valued description. But there is a way out, because in fact we are not that description. We do not have to have a valued description in order to be real and to be happy. All those descriptions are mere combinations of appearances in our experience. They change constantly, falling into now this pattern, now that, like fragments of color in a kaleidoscope. *That's* not what we mean by a *real self*. The real self is what is back of all those de-scriptions, quite independent of them. Nor is it the possessor of the descriptions. It itself has no description. There is nothing you can say to define it. You cannot refer it to some other being and say it bears this relation to that being, and that tells what it is. You cannot compare it with another being and say it is better or worse or bigger or smaller. As long as we remain accustomed to thinking that reality is whatever can be defined or described—whatever has attributes and can be related and compared to other beings—this Real Self looks to us like nothing at all: it is emptiness, a void, a No-Self, a big zero.

Indeed, the sages say that all we can say of it, in terms of our descriptive experience, is that it is *Neti, Neti*, not this, not that; it is *Nirguna*, without attributes, not composed of strands woven together as all descriptive beings are. Not being a descriptive or defined being, it has no need or desire to enhance its description; it has no fire of craving for more and better attributes. That fire has died out: Nirvana. The Western saint, too, who proceeds by the *via negativa*, who enters the cloud of unknowing, who strips the soul of all descriptive goods and qualities, knows that one comes in contact with Deep Reality only when one reaches this central Nothing, this *Nada*.

This sense of nothing, of emptiness, is only the last of the appearances in the world of contrast perception. It is in comparison with descriptive being that the real self appears to be empty and to be nothing. As a descriptive being, a being defined and known by its attributes and its essence, it is truly a nothing, and nothing can be said of it. But it *is* experienced, and vividly experienced, as the true reality, as fullness of being, as activity of existence. We cannot look at it from outside, for from there we can see only descriptions. It must be experienced from the inside, by actually *being* it. It is sheer I AM, without adding "I am this," or "I am that." No, only "I am who I am." The children of God bear the Name of the Parent, and if they would be true, they must take care not to take that Name in vain.

Thinking of ourselves in this way enables us to experience ourselves as existence, as act, instead of looking at ourselves as essence, as substance. It suggests that we experience ourselves as verbs rather than as nouns, as interflowing processes of living rather than as bounded and separated entities. If our sense of being, of being real, and being good, is not a sense of *what* we are but *that* we are, a sense of existing and acting that is independent of the descriptions through which our particular actions take place, then we begin to get a new picture of reality. Now contrast is not needed to give value, because the value lies in the act of existing itself, and it is *this act which we are*, a far greater thing than any description in which we might be clothed. "Why," asked Jesus, "are you worried about how you will be clothed? Life is far greater than clothing."

This is only the beginning. The realization of the true self as transcendent of all descriptions, as free of the need to identify or value itself by contrast, as being the act of existing, as inheriting the name of God, I AM, is only the first step in working out the metaphysics of the children of God.

To Be Children of God Is to Be Love

"Let us love one another, for love is of God, and whoever loves is born of God . . . for God is love." —1 John 4:7–8

In order to explain this idea of love properly, we must go more deeply into the psychology of the true self. The central point is that to experience the true self we must coincide consciously with the act of existing and not be thinking *about* ourselves. The self that we think about is a particular entity possessed of various attributes, and it is these attributes that we actually think about when we consider that self. Furthermore, thinking about ourselves makes us treat ourselves as objects of knowledge and turns us into split beings: subjects who know and objects that are known. This is the basic form of dualism that all spiritual traditions urge us to avoid. "Let your eye be single," they recommend; "then your whole being will be illumined."

Padma Sambhava, who brought Buddhism to Tibet in the eighth century, said:

> There are not two such things as sought and seeker . . . ; when fully comprehended, the sought is found to be one with the seeker. If the seeker . . . when sought, cannot be found, thereupon is attained the goal of the seeking and also the end of the search itself.[4]

It is that which the eye cannot see when it looks for itself. An eye attempting to see itself is an eye trying to double itself. When the eye realizes that it *is* the eye, *is* the seer, then the eye is single, and that is Illumination, that is Enlightenment.

Wei Wu Wei, who draws on Vedanta, as well as Taoism and Zen, puts it this way:

> Although [Original Consciousness] is all that [people] are—and despite the fact that in it, therefore, they have nothing to attain, grasp or possess—[nevertheless] in order that they may "live" it, [as distinguished from] having objective understanding of what it is, . . . they must *de-phenomenalise themselves*, dis-objectify themselves, dis-identify their Subjectivity from its projected phenomenal selfhood. . . . This displacement of subjectivity is from apparent object to ultimate subject in which it inheres, . . . from supposed individual to universal absolute.[5]

Therefore, we should try to coincide with ourselves as the act of existing that we are, with that fountain of living energy that springs up in the midst of us and actually *is* eternal life.[6] This sense of sheer existence, before the attention is directed to some object, has no form and hence no limitation. It is in this sense that we may call it infinite. It is existence, not essence; it is formless, not formed; it transcends time and space; and it is experienced by coinciding with it noetically, not by thinking *about* it or knowing it as an object.

This formless existence-self is active, not passive. It is experienced as coincidence, or confluence, with the fountain of eternal life in our heart. We are this springing up, this flowing out. It is our own act of living. When we consciously unite with it, it is also our will. This is the fundamental meaning of uniting one's will to the will of God. We feel it as an act in which we are engaged. It is process; it is motion; it is flow; it is radiation.

Notice that whenever our attention is engaged passively, as distinguished from this sense of sheer active existence, what we are doing is re-acting, re-sponding. The action has begun outside us, somewhere in the environment. Something has presented itself to be noticed, to be known, to be valued, to be acted upon. We may attend or not attend; we may award positive or negative value—that is, like or dislike; we may elect to act or not act, to act in this way or that way. But all these alternatives have been *presented by the environment* and offered to our attention and our will for *choice*. The environment has also put pressure on us in one way or another to claim our attention and our choice. The situation is characterized by *passive attention* because we are passive to the actions of the environment on us. And it is characterized by *choice freedom*. We are free to make choices among the alternatives offered us by the environment. When we make these choices and engage our will in these responses, we do so because of the qualities in the situation presented by the environment and the relation that these qualities bear to certain qualities in our attribute-self. For instance, we love people who please us, do us good, are friendly to us.

In order to be able to love people who do not please us, do not do us good, are not friendly to us, we must take some other stance. We may say to ourselves that after all they are human beings too and on that ground deserving of our love, regardless of how they behave toward us. Or we may say that our religious leader has claimed identity with them and asked us to love them, and for the sake of that obligation, we will strive to do so. But in these cases we are still giving reasons for the love. Something outside ourselves stimulates and calls forth the love. We are still passive.

In order to love without regard to whether the beloved is worthy or unworthy, without any motive arising from the environment, in order to love as an original and authoritative act, we must situate ourselves at a still deeper source of freedom. Beyond choice freedom there is *creative freedom*, which is grounded in *active attention*, the sense of simply coinciding with existing as a unitary outflowing act.

Choice freedom is a response to a stimulus from the environment; creative freedom acts from itself alone, not as a response, not as a re-action, but as an original act, proceeding only from itself as a first cause. It is called "creative" because it creates as it acts. The passive, or responsive, lover first finds an object worthy of love and then loves. The active, or creative, lover first loves and then there is a beloved.[7]

The self that can do this is the existential formless self. The self composed of descriptions can only engage in motivated love in terms of relations between itself and those loved. This is why we find it so difficult to love all our neighbors. Our emotions respond only to people and situations that please and benefit us. As Jesus said, anybody can do that. If we want to live the divine life, as befits children of God, we must learn to love the way God loves—creatively, originally, not because those loved deserve it, or are attractive, pleasing, or beneficial. Nor because they *fail* to have these characteristics, and we can be grandly virtuous by loving our enemies. Divine love doesn't have any "because." It is itself the original act and is not referred elsewhere for an account of itself. Long before there is a "because" in the world, God loves. The act of being God is the act of loving—and this loving creates the world.

If we are really children of God, we are capable of entering into this kind of love. In fact, we must fundamentally and centrally *be* this kind of love, if it is true that we are children of God. Just as we must each be a pure I AM, transcendent of all descriptive predicates, so this very I AM must be a great outpouring Fiat, MAY YOU BE, a radiating love-energy. Our attitude toward all other beings will be the will that they may be, and may be fully, abundantly.[8]

A disciple of the Buddha came to him one day and said, "It seems to me that love and friendliness are a great part of the illuminated life." "You are wrong," said the Buddha. "Love and friendliness are *all* of the illuminated life."

In this way another chain reaction is set up, which is just the opposite of the sin chain, in which each injured party hurt another in an attempt to regain the sense of superiority that was equated with well-being. In the love chain, the lover is free from any need to establish self-esteem and so has abundant energy to expend on others. This affirming energy, entering into the beloved, will—if accepted—so liberate the beloved from the need to maintain contrast relationships in order to feel good that the beloved will also be free to devote excess energy to loving still others. As the Buddha said, "Hatred does not cease by hatred at any time: hatred ceases by love."[9]

This is what happens when the Enlightened One acts as a Bodhisattva, when the Baptized One acts as a Savior. This is how we can discover community based not on interdependence, the sharing of lacks, but on superabundance. We have great reserves of personal energy, but they are presently employed in ego-defense. Once this energy is liberated, we will have enormous amounts of personal love-energy to share with all. There is no necessary scarcity of love.

Notice that the lover, acting out of the formless existential self, does not say (as a descriptive self would), "I am I insofar as I am different from you, insofar as I am not you," but "I am I precisely insofar as I give myself to you, live in you, unite with you." We see, then, that love does two things simultaneously: it both differentiates and unites. There is differentiation because what love *is* is the outgoing energy from one to another. But what does this outgoing act do? It unites with that other. And the more a lover goes out in love to unite with the other, the more the lover is established as a lover. The more I give myself away in love, the more I become myself, because that's what I *am*, a lover.

Their having a different collection of attributes does not distinguish lover and beloved. The act of creative loving itself establishes their existential differentiation—for the beloved will also be a lover in turn—and establishes this differentiation at the same time that it establishes union.

This is how we begin to develop our new method of organizing and appreciating our experience. Crucial to it is a new way of differentiating or distinguishing ourselves. We had been doing it by comparison; now we can glimpse how it can be done out of a sense of an existential formless selfhood that acts with creative freedom to love all.

To Be Children of God Is to Be Perichoresis

"In that day you will know that I am in my Father, and you in me, and I in you." —John 14:20

"I pray . . . that they may all be one . . . even as . . . we are one." —John 17:22

As we saw in chapter 4, *perichoresis*, the traditional Greek word for the activity of the Trinity, refers primarily to the way the Persons live in one another. It is particularly strong in the traditions of the

Orthodox Church. According to James and Myfanwy Moran, "Orthodoxy believes that . . . in the Holy Trinity the divine life is conferred on and shared by the three persons only because they give it one to another out of love: divine life is a personal offering between them, given and received freely."[10] This is a great clue and helps us to resolve what has been perceived as the problem of nondualism.

The Eastern traditions, for the most part, insist that when one is fully enlightened, there is no longer a distinction between "me" and "my environment." The basic dualism of subject and object has been transcended and therefore all the other perceptions, conceptions, and values according to contrast and preference also have been overcome. (One can, of course, still see a black cow standing in a snowfield and understand how a circle differs from a square.) When consciousness is *limited* to the passive mode of receiving what is presented to it by the environment, there must be a distinction between it and the environment and distinctions among the various items in the environment. But when the consciousness, by concentrating its attention in the active mode, coincides with its own act of existing, the fragmentation of the world as experienced stops, and one is aware of unity with the whole.[11]

The West treasures individual personality, and worries that the individual personality might be lost in such a nondual experience. Our insight into the nature of love should enable us to resolve this difficulty. First, we should distinguish between "personality" and "person." Personality refers to the phenomenal observation we make of one another according to descriptions of attributes: Somebody has a particular temperament or disposition or constellation of behaviors. This, clearly, belongs to the fragmented world in which contrast and preference rule.

Person, on the other hand, refers to the living one who transcends those descriptions and is simply the act of existing as a flowing fountain of consciousness. This person is able to love with creative freedom, to love all equally without preference or privilege, above contrast and conflict. When we realize ourselves as persons, we do not cling to our personalities—although we still have them—and do not insist that the success, superiority, and satisfaction of our personalities determine the value of our life. Because we are not judging everything by reference to our self-esteem, we are free to love, to will the being and well-being of others.

This act of love, we have said, simultaneously establishes union and differentiation. The person who loves cannot be lost in some vague sea of generalized being, because the context is no longer essence but existence. Fear of absorption into the Whole is secretly based on a metaphysical view that sees all reality as composed of different substances distinguished from one another by their respective attributes. Since the possession of mutually negating attributes is considered in that view to be all that keeps these substances distinct from one another, if the attributes are taken away, the beings will all collapse into an undifferentiated mush.

But if the person is defined as the activity of existing, and one is oneself through acts of creative freedom projecting love-energies toward other persons, there is no possibility that anyone will be lost in some general fusion of All. There cannot be such a fusion into any simplistic unity because the lovers are distinct by their acts of loving. *This distinctness is original,* just as the act of creative loving is original and does not depend on the worthiness of the beloved. One starts with the distinctness in the existence itself, a distinctness not dependent on the possession of attributes that are different from those of others: The person *is* a lover; a lover *is* the act of loving; the act of loving establishes differentiation simultaneously with union.

Nevertheless, this union is total. That is the *perichoresis.* Each loving person is thoroughly "in" each other loving person. There is nothing to prevent it. The two persons are not different from one another because they possess mutually exclusive attributes: they are distinct because they are their own acts of existing. But what does love desire and intend? It wants to give itself completely to the beloved and so unite with the other as to live in the other's own life. The lover is not satisfied with knowing about the beloved from afar. The lover wants to know the beloved, to understand the beloved, to feel with the beloved.

Let me put this in terms of our language. When we talk about someone, someone who is not present, we say "her" or "him." There is a definite sense of absence and separation in the I-it, I-her, I-him, we-them relation. But when the person spoken about comes into our presence, our whole consciousness changes. We say "you" to the person and everything feels very different. We somehow enter into that other person, and we let the other enter into us. We engage one another. Something of what is myself becomes involved with what is yourself.

But this I-Thou relation is still not the ultimate union. This face-to-face encounter is not fully satisfying to love. Love wants to share in everything of the beloved's life and wants to give its entire life to the beloved. It wants to experience what the beloved experiences, from the beloved's own point of view, and to permit the beloved to share the lover's life with the same fullness. What love really wants is to enter into the beloved and coincide with the beloved's own subjectivity. This ultimate relation of love we may therefore call the I-I relation.

It is not a face-to-face encounter. It is a coincidence of two subjects, both facing the same way. One does not know or love the other as a subject knows or loves an object. One unites with the other to the extent of coinciding with that person from the inside, experiencing what it is to be that person from the subject side. This is the union properly called "mystical." William Shannon, commenting on Thomas Merton's experience and writings, puts it concisely: "In contemplation . . . the subjectivity of the contemplative becomes one with the subjectivity of God."[12] Each subject thus sees through the other's eyes, feels with the other's heart, wills in conjunction with the other's will, and flows together with the other's action.

There is now no sense of outsideness at all, no sense of separation. Each one dwells "in" the other. But each continues to feel clearly "I am I," for the subjective act of existing is what each subject is.

An image may help. Consider two spotlights playing on a stage floor. You see two pools of light at the ends of the two beams. Then the two spots move toward one another, partly overlap, overlap more, and finally coincide; there is now only one circle of light on the floor. But each of the two beams is playing into the one circle. With respect to that circle of light, each of the two beams can correctly say, "It is I."

In this relation, the subjective sense of being one's true self is not lost or blurred, but actually strengthened, for one feels fulfilled in one's inmost nature as an unlimited, undefined person who is a self-giving lover.

This is ec-stasy, passing out of oneself to enter into the other, there to be as the other. This means en-stasy, passing into the other's own self-realization. But what is the other's enstasy, the other's self-realization? Why, it is again that the other is also an undefined person and a creative lover, also passing out in ecstasy to unite with the enstatic self-realization of still a third person. Thus our first lover, in uniting with the second, unites with what is the very heart of that person's being and action, namely that person's outgoing love for the third, and so on. In this experience, both models of spiritual life, that which culminates in ecstasy and that which culminates in enstasy, can be verified.

This subject-subject coinherence—this I-I relation—achieves the perfection of personal integrity at the same time that it overcomes duality. It offers us a model of nondualism that is also *perichoresis,* uniting a basic insight of the East with a fundamental value of the West. If *perichoresis*—the way the Divine Persons are conceived as giving themselves totally to one another and thereby constituting their unity—is a valid view of God, and we embrace the assertion that we are children of God, we arrive at a powerful image of what human community could be.

We too can each of us be a unique whole person whose existential reality flows out in ecstatic and creative love to other persons and so deeply bonds with them that in our confluent activity we are one living being. The image of the unitary living body has often been applied to the human race, and stories of the dismembered divinity have offered mythic explanations of our fragmentation relative to our original and true nature. The *perichoresis* image preserves a vivid sense of individual personal subjective existence without weakening the unity that is not only our political aspiration but what mystics of all cultures affirm as our ultimate reality.

Here we find that inter-independence based on superabundance that can replace even the best interdependence based on scarcity and deprivation. Note that this attitude, this personal orientation, does not mean that the earth will not run short of oil or clean water; it does, however, imply that we can deal with such problems more freely and creatively than is possible given our present mentality. Inter-independence understands sharing, not as a need imposed by scarcity, but as a value in itself.

When there is a felt sense of one's life being in all equally, there is firm motivation to develop, to garner, to distribute, and to conserve for the benefit of the Whole, for each of us says, "I am the Whole." We do not have to struggle to balance our several greeds and hold our national self-interests in some equilibrium of power; we can live in a genuine community. Only because we lack a spontaneous perception of ourselves as a living Whole do we continue with our current destructive struggles.

To try to reach politically negotiated arrangements, or even to preach morally inspired sharing, is not enough because our basic perception would still be one of scarcity, of loss, of sacrifice. We need a new sense of self-being as full of abundant life; we need the capacity to share that life as a free and joyous natural act.

This can come about only by first realizing ourselves as transcendent and then by identifying ourselves with the Whole. But we must not lose the sense of the unique personal integrity of each subject. The model of *perichoresis* offers a way to have a sense of ourselves both as subjective centers of living reality and as totally united with all by our own free and personal act.

To Be Children of God Is to Be Incarnate as Creative Process

"The Word became flesh and dwelt among us, full of grace and truth."
    —John 1:14

"My word . . . that goes forth from my mouth . . . shall not return to me empty, but it shall . . . prosper in the thing for which I sent it."
    —Isa. 46:11

All that has been said so far has stressed the transcendent character of what has been called our true selves. This had to be clearly understood and established first so that the incarnate aspect of this global spirituality for the future could be properly presented as a creative process. Once we experience ourselves in terms of existence rather than essence, as active rather than passive, as undefined and incomparable, full and free and in loving union with all, we are able to appreciate our incarnate expression as beauty and art rather than as limitation and restriction.

Let us use the imagery of Trinitarian theology once more, this time from another point of view. The root of reality is called the Source or Parent of all, and it is conceived as expressing itself by breathing forth a meaning, a Word. The Word is, so to speak, the form that the Holy Breath takes as it issues from the Source. The Word is further seen as taking on flesh in the human world: the self-expression of Infinite Being takes a finite form. It does not lose its infinitude by so doing. That full reality, the incarnate Deity, is both infinite and finite, both formless and possessed of form.

This is also the message of Hindu and Buddhist teaching. Brahman, the Ultimate Reality, is both *Nirguna,* without finite form, not composed, and also *Saguna,* with finite composed forms. The enlightened Buddhist realizes that Nirvana, the state of transcendence, is actually not different from samsara, the world of process and particularity. One's reality belongs to both simultaneously. Both traditions alert us to the important fact that spiritual life does not end with the mystic experience of union with the Absolute. Rather, that is where it begins. Once we have properly grasped our transcendent and incomparable reality, we are ready to live a creative life, as children of a creative God should do.

Our incarnate life in the world is a process: it flows, it improvises like a skillful musician, it creates a work of art. When our consciousness enters completely into the realization of ourselves as free to love all equally and to unite with the whole, we experience the artistic development of the human process and the world process as fulfilling the divine creative act. This will include all types and levels of our human activity, our economic and ecological arrangements, our social relations, our scientific and technical exploration and invention, our artistic expressions.

Perichoresis suggests a new model for organization in these enterprises, one that preserves differentiation by existential act while entering into a profound and thorough union with all. There are other

images being developed now that do a similar thing. Their constellation indicates that already our consciousness is turning in this direction. David Bohm has proposed the implicate order as foundation
for the various explicate systems that appear to our observation. Karl
Pribram has popularized the hologram as a metaphor for the way the
least particle of the whole nevertheless contains the whole. Fritjof
Capra has taken up the nondualistic philosophies of the East and
argued their compatibility with contemporary physics. All these
schemes have in common the abandonment of the separate-entity
concept of individual being. In some way each of them suggests that
what is from one point of view a *part*, is from another point of view,
the *whole*.[13] This is the sort of spontaneous perception of our being
that we need in order to create our united world of the future.

These thinkers have made useful suggestions because they have
dared to try something completely different. They have studied
the basic assumptions of the old systems and asked, "What if we made
some other assumption?" All creation has to be courageous enough to
do just this. We have to understand that loyalty goes first to life itself
and not to our received ideas about life. The Angel of the Resurrection reminds us not to seek the Living One among the dead.

Thus, although vigorous protest against old structures that limit
or violate the dignity of the human person is certainly in order, what
is even better is simply to turn away from these structures wherever
possible and set about creating and demonstrating new ones. This is
the call of the future: "Let us go where we have never been before!" If
we are truly children of God, this is surely a most appropriate thing
for us to do as our inheritance from the God who says, "Behold, I
make all things new!"

And so, after withdrawing from our sense of limited identity with
a restricted self, after realization of our transcendence and freedom
and our nature as ecstatic lovers who enter into the profound union of
the nondual *perichoresis*, we turn our faces outward again in the creative process of incarnation. Let us note, as a final image of this life of
ours, that after the death of the old perceptions, and after the Sabbath
rest in the realization of transcendence,[14] we come into the Resurrection, which takes place on the first day of a new working week.

Notes

1. Hoyle mentioned his prediction again in a speech to the Apollo 11 Lunar Science Conference, January 6, 1970, in Houston. Cited in Donald D. Clayton, *The Dark Night Sky* (New York: Quadrangle/N.Y. Times Book Co., 1975), p. 127.

2. Matt. 23:8–9; 20:25–26.

3. Mark 1:11.

4. Cited in Ken Wilber, *The Spectrum of Consciousness* (Wheaton, IL: Theosophical Publishing House, 1977), p. 334.

5. Ibid., pp. 331–332.

6. Cf. John 4:14.

7. Cf. John 4:19.

8. Cf. Gen. 1:3; John 10:10.

9. The Dhammapada. See, e.g., Eknath Easwaran, *God Makes the Rivers to Flow* (Petaluma, CA: Nilgiri Press, 1982), p. 32.

10. *Parabola*, vol. 7, no. 4, p. 53.

11. Wilber, pp. 314–315.

12. William H. Shannon, *Thomas Merton's Dark Path: The Inner Experience of a Contemplative* (New York: Penguin, 1982), p. 223.

13. See David Bohm, *Wholeness and the Implicate Order* (London: Routledge and Kegan Paul, 1980); Fritjof Capra, *The Tao of Physics* (Boulder, CO: Shambhala, 1975); Karl H. Pribram, "Holonomy and Structure in the Organization of Perception," in J. M. Nicholas, ed., *Images, Perception, and Knowledge* (Dordrecht: Reidel, 1977), and see Ken Wilber, ed., *The Holographic Paradigm and Other Paradoxes* (Boulder, CO: Shambhala, 1982). See also Robert Nadeau and Menas Kafatos, *The Non-Local Universe: The New Physics and Matters of the Mind* (New York: Oxford, 1999).

14. For development of this image, see the author's *The Easter Mysteries* (New York: Crossroad, 1995), chapter 8.

EIGHT

The Living One

Transcendent Freedom Creates
the Future

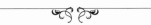

"Then I saw a new heaven and a new earth."
—Rev. 21:1

The Angel of the Resurrection said to the women who came to the tomb, "Why do you seek the Living One among the dead?" It is a question that cuts to the heart of our sense of reality. Do we not all persist in doing what those good women were doing? Questing after Reality, do we not faithfully make our way to the region of the dead past, hoping to be able to embalm the remains that rest there and guard them against the corruption of life, against the worm and the microbe that will break down those forms and make their energies available to new forms and new processes?

Despite our best efforts, life does eat through the shells of the dead and press its way forward into the future. The Angel of the Resurrection, the Messenger of the Renewal of Life, says, "If you want to find the Living One, you must not look among the dead." The Living One is never in the remains of the past but always on the verge of the future. Believing in the Resurrection, entering into the Resurrection, means rearranging our sense of reality to see the world this way. Mythically rendered, this is the theme that I wish to explore now.

Earlier chapters have developed concepts and arguments that to some degree I presuppose and extend here. Those chapters urged that we are undergoing a critical moment in our evolution as human beings, one in which "feminine" values of wholeness, unity, and synthesis will integrate the "masculine" values of abstraction, specialization, and distinction into a new and higher level of consciousness. The new consciousness moves us away from the "domination paradigm" of human society, which has characterized most of our thinking and our behavior up to now, and toward a "communion paradigm." The mythic representation of this shift is the dual event of Holy Thursday: the destruction of the lord/servant relationship by Jesus' act of washing his disciples' feet, and the institution of the communion relationship by the sharing of the Sacred Supper. The communion consciousness unites the members of its community by a self-giving love that simultaneously grounds the identity of each unique person in the community and brings into being the New Creation as an image of the Trinity.

The present chapter, having reviewed quickly the notions of the transcendent person as the "living one" who exists in radical and creative freedom, will undertake to push this line of thought further by contemplating the act of living as the projection of free, creative, love-energies at the mysterious frontier between the present and the future. It will be suggested that where we really live is not in the fixed forms of the past but on the verge of the future, a future genuinely nonexistent and unknowable, a future of radical novelty created by improvisation. This way of locating the act of living will help us to gain a revolutionary sense of the reality of the person as creative process and as "interpersonhood" and, thus, to see ourselves as a holy community that is the created and creating image of the interpersonhood of the Trinity, the archetypal Living One.

Transcendent Personhood

The notion and the image of "the Living One" first came up, in the development of this thought, in connection with the question of forgiveness. Neo-feminine communion consciousness was supposed to be established as "mutual affirmation" in which each person experienced self-identity by saying, "I am I insofar as I am in you," instead of the mutual negation "I am I insofar as I am not you." But this projection of positive energies toward another person might appear to be very difficult in the case where the persons were separated by serious injury and injustice.

The difficulty was resolved by pointing out that the affirmation is addressed to the person where that person is actually living now, not to what the person had done in the past. If we relate ourselves only to the past deeds of others, we will always be at least one step behind where they themselves presently are, and thus we will never really be in relationship with *them*, but only with their "remains."

Rather, our act of living affirmation must be addressed to the other living person just at the point where that person is in the act of creating the next moment of life. Our well-wishing, our intention to give life and give it abundantly, unites with the other's creative act of stepping forward into the next moment. We give forward into the future, for the sake of the future, a future necessarily unknown, subject to free creativity. This is the essence of forgiveness. It is not a statement about the past. It is an act of making the future.

Viewed this way, the essence of *forgiveness* is simply the essence of love in general, the energetic radiation of a good will for the sake of the future. This "intensified giving," which "gives" itself "away," is the heart of agape. We have limited the signification of "forgiveness" to those situations in which we have found it psychologically most difficult to practice love, but its literal and root meaning is far broader. This casts an interesting light on the role of the rites of forgiveness and reconciliation in the Christian liturgy, especially their position as preparatory to the celebration of the community's unity in image of the Trinity's unity.

In our ordinary daily life, we find forgiveness psychologically difficult. Psychologically, we identify other people with their pasts and identify ourselves with our own past. We have images of our respective personalities and characters, built up from an accumulation of past experiences. We argue, with plentiful evidence, that we may expect future behaviors and attitudes to be like those of the past. And so we claim to be justified in continuing our negative feelings toward those with whom we have had unpleasant experiences.

All perfectly true on its own level, which we are calling here the "psychological" level. But this is the level of the dead, in our mythic language. We are relating the deadness of ourselves, of our past and of our fixed and bounded shell of being, to the deadness of the others, to their pasts and defined, bounded beings. In the myth, the Living One addresses us on this subject, saying, "Let the dead bury their dead. You come, walk with me." There is a place for the relations of the dead to the dead. That is part of the world, too. But we will not find the Living One there.

The Living One, the Vivificator, is spirit. Its activities do not take place on the psychological level. This is a distinction that is very important to grasp and is missed by many. We have a great tendency to confuse the spiritual with the psychological, with feelings and emotions. The spirit is the living essence of the self, transcendent of the particular traits that compose what we call the personality. The defined elements of our personalities, like other defined beings, properly identify themselves by mutual negation, by not-being one another. But *person* is not a defined being, not a personality. Person is unbounded activity of freely projecting subjective energies. It transcends all descriptions, all the categories under which "we" can be classified according to our dead "remains."

If we attend very carefully to our sense of being alive, of being real, and gradually eliminate all sense of identification by any categorical description, we will find ourselves profoundly centered in a sense of sheer "I am." However, immediately upon this discovery, we also realize that this deep center, "I am," is radiating in all directions the intention "May you be!" This is the transcendent person in the act of living its spiritual life. The affirmation which is *agape*, the will that another should live abundantly, the act of forgiveness, is directed by this transcendent spiritual person toward another transcendent spiritual person.

We say that we are created in the image of God. This is where that image is to be found. The image lies in our being undefined, active, free subjects. It further lies in our being *inter*personal, *inter*subjective. As persons we identify ourselves by our mutual affirmation, the beaming of life and love energies into one another so that our very selfhood dwells in those who are affirmed. We say we give *ourselves* to those we love. This must be understood literally. It is our selfhood that we give, that we exchange. This is how we become the image of the Trinity.

In saying these things, we need constantly to guard against reverting to thinking of ourselves as being our personalities, our traits and talents, our feelings, our emotions, our history and our past, the biography that is called by our name. If we identify with the personality, we will not understand correctly the meaning of self-giving. Everything turns on the identity of the self, what we mean when we say "I." The location of our sense of reality is the crucial point in the passage from the psychological level to the spiritual level. This is the *metanoia* that is involved in the elevation of consciousness that takes place in the Holy Thursday revolution.

The emotional personality may *feel like* life to us. The life-story that is called by our name may seem to be our only way of *conceptualizing* our life. This is why it seems that we would be losing our life if we were to give up identifying ourselves in these ways. The *metanoia* is said to be like dying and being reborn. It is a shift in our sense of real being, our sense of being alive, from the emotional personality to the transcendent spirit. The first level human being may be described as a living soul, but the next level human being is to be a life-giving spirit. All the practices of the ascetical life are aimed at helping us make this transition. By seeming to die, we release ourselves from identification with the dead, and by realizing ourselves as transcendent persons, we establish ourselves in true life and can begin to do truly living, that is to say, divine, things.

Creative Freedom

The clue to transcendent selfhood is freedom. The actions of a person are said to be free because they are determined by the acting person, the agent, not by another. Usually we understand this as meaning that we can make a choice among different courses of action or different attitudes toward a situation, or even a choice between acting and not acting. Nothing forces us to make the choice that we make; our act of choosing is not the effect of a cause outside ourselves. Nevertheless, this *choice freedom*, as we have called it, is a comparatively limited freedom, because both the alternatives and the stimulation to make a choice among them originate in the environment, not in the agent.

There is a deeper freedom, which we have called transcendent freedom, or *creative freedom*. It is not stimulated to act by some item in the environment. The action begins with the agent as its first source. The agent exercises an initiative. Similarly, the type of action that the agent undertakes is not limited by a set of alternatives presented by the environment. The act is strictly creative; it determines its own nature and originates itself as existing. It is not a reaction, not a response to a stimulus from without.

This is easy enough to see in the distinction between love as eros and love as agape. Eros is a response to some merit or goodness in the beloved. It is also a matter of valuing the beloved for the sake of the good that the beloved can offer the lover. Even a very "high-minded" love, such as love of a teacher or guide because that individual helps one to become wise or holy, is erotic love. It is the parallel to choice freedom, a response to a value already present in the environment.

Agape, by contrast, does not value the beloved for the sake of the lover but strictly for the beloved's own sake. This does not mean that agape is a response to some merit in the beloved. It does not love the beloved because the beloved is *already* good but in order that the beloved may *become* good—where "good" refers to every kind of value, including existence. Agape is a "prevenient grace"; it precedes its object. It is as though one first loves and *then* the beloved comes into being or into value subsequently. That is to say, agape's own orientation and attitude are creative: it wills to give abundantly to the beloved. It throws its own being into its will to give to the beloved.

Like forgiveness, agape is an exercise of creative freedom and is future oriented. It addresses itself to what does not yet exist. It is even more than a contemplative or appreciative love, which admires and savors the beloved without asking anything from it or attempting to add anything to it. Agape is active; it bursts with energetic desire that there be more being.

This is the characteristic of transcendent selfhood. Whenever we are uncertain whether we are living on the psychological level or the spiritual level, a good test is to see how much freedom we are exercising. If we find that we are identifying ourselves with our inability to resist certain negative emotions, or with the state in which waves of positive feelings sweep over us unbidden, then we are not identifying ourselves with our freedom and are living only on the psychological, not the spiritual, level.

If we consciously respond to the world by deliberately choosing to behave in certain ways, that is a degree of freedom. Such acts may be either good or evil. It is important to note that it is more "spiritual" to do good freely than to be carried away by positive emotions. Spirituality is identified by activity, not passivity, by initiative, not helplessness. Moreover, evil acts can never be of the order of creative freedom, because they are always chosen in reference to some good for the one choosing; that is, they are always responsive, not purely originative.

Full freedom and spirituality are reached when we originate and initiate acts of creative self-giving, without any passivity. Such acts are truly spontaneous, being done by us as their authors. We may remark in passing that most of us resist freedom and creativity. We like to insist on the importance of passivity, on having things done to us. We make mystiques out of our helplessness and our incapacity. Of course, it is only right not to attribute to a level or type of being an activity or a responsibility that it cannot in fact support. But we might do well to reflect a bit on the eagerness with which we disclaim power, authorship, and consequently responsibility, as evolvers of our own beings and as co-creators of our world.

It is only the transcendent selfhood that can exercise creative freedom. The personality, defined by its descriptions, which set it off from other personalities, is obliged by its very constitution to protect its being by defending its descriptions. It must practice erotic love in order to sustain and enlarge itself. It responds to and utilizes the environment in its operation of nurturing its descriptive being. Thus it can never go beyond choice freedom.

The self that transcends the descriptions has nothing to defend or protect. Its whole being consists precisely of giving itself away, so it has nothing to lose. The more it despoils itself, the richer it grows. All its energy moves out from it in order to make more being in the world, and this movement begins in the transcendent self. This is the sense in which it is free, spontaneous, and creative. This is the intensified sense of being alive, of centering oneself in the act of living, which is synonymous with the act of creating: it is the same transcendent self that says "I am" and "May you be!"

The Act of Living

An image that comes readily to mind in the attempt to describe the shift of consciousness from the dead past to the living moment is that of the coral. What do we usually think of when we meet the word "coral"? A kind of pinkish stone that is found in reefs or on beaches and can be polished and set into jewelry—isn't that what springs first to our imagination? Unless, of course, one happens to be a biologist, a close student of life. The biologist knows that "coral" really means the little animal, called a polyp, that leaves behind this stony mass that had been its skeleton. The polyp itself is not hard and fixed; it is a mass of soft, moving protoplasm, interacting with its environment, like any other living being. But this is an afterthought—almost a curiosity—to us. What we think of when we say "coral" is the stone.

It is the same way when we think of our own lives, or the world, or the meanings we attach to our lives. We tend first to think of them as static, fixed, externalized, accumulated matter. We build up our lives as the coral builds up its reef and then we think of our self as the reef rather than as the living act that from moment to moment is adding on to the reef. The world is a similar structure, whose real being to us is the accumulation of its externalized past. We would find it quite exotic—and certainly impractical—to think of the world as making itself from moment to moment and to consider that if we are to relate to it, we must catch it in the act, just as the next moment is coming into existence. The meanings we give our lives in the world are values attached to certain arrangements of these facts about the past, and we are loath to see any of them change. To suppose that we can, let alone must, freely and responsibly create our meaning from moment to moment as we go along is profoundly disturbing.

And yet, real life exists only in the moment of living. What is left as the product of the act of living is something cast off, refuse. Such products are real enough; that is not contested. They also have values appropriate to them; this is not denied. But where shall we, as spiritual beings, set our primary sense of reality? That is the question. We are so accustomed to thinking about the large blocks of reality that can be neatly formed and categorized, either as past or as fantasized future, that we require a deliberate effort and a set of specialized techniques to enable us to center our consciousness into the present moment and contact the reality of the act of living.

We go to a spiritual teacher and pour forth our feelings about what is happening to us in our life, all our memories and our expectations. The teacher says, "Hush! Just be here now." And we can't do it. It seems to us to be nothing. We are so habituated to the artificial reality of remembered past and fantasized future (which is only projected and manipulated past), that we have no taste for the integral reality of the present moment. We do not know what to look for in it.

The teacher may point out two things to look for: emptiness and novelty. Emptiness means that all the categories are dissolved. The living moment does not itself fall into any category; it is the creator of categories. It does not have a defined form, because it is the generator of forms. In our consciousness it is the "I am" as distinct from the "me," the objectified self identified by its description.

Novelty means that each succeeding moment is fresh, is genuinely new, is not a rerun. We tend to greet every moment as a repeat of the general forms of the past, or even to assume that we are existing in the midst of a great "still," not a moving picture at all. There is a sense in which we do not realize that we are alive. We spend our days among the dead, recording the inscriptions on the tombstones. The spiritual teachers try to break us out of this limited consciousness into a new world that they call being Awake, or Risen from the Dead.

When we are able to center ourselves in the act of living, the teacher may point out two more things to us. One is the radiant character of life. We have already spoken of this as the "I am" that is coincident with the "May you be," and as the love called agape.

Another way of saying it is to call our act of living a radiation of "spondic energy," energy that is poured out as an act of reverence or worship. We realize ourselves as like radiance pouring out, like the stars, like the sun, a luminous being that radiates itself in all directions mightily.

Spondic energy is the energy of the spiritual will. It is not an urge; it is not desire. It is not a warm feeling. It is not a cold feeling, either. It is not a matter of feeling at all, because it is not passive, not something that happens to us. It is a matter of free intention. It is our self, under our own control. The radiation of spondic energy is a deliberate act on our part, performed by our consciousness in full realization of what it is doing. It is a prime example of creative freedom as distinct from choice freedom. There is no choice here, even of whether to do it or not to do it, yet the act is profoundly and purely free. It is only and originally *our* act, our act of living.

The other thing that the spiritual teacher may point out is the mutual indwelling that goes on among all the living consciousnesses. As undefined and radiant beings, we do not identify ourselves with any boundaries. As creatively loving beings, we pour ourselves into others' lives—not into their descriptions and personalities, or their histories, we must remind ourselves, but into their transcendent acts of living. And the other, similarly radiant and loving beings, pour their lives into ours. It is no longer clear where the *edges* of our beings are. This does not mean that there is confusion or obliteration of unique personhood. It is perfectly clear where one's *center* is: it is the origin of the personal radiant energy that is freely pouring out and mingling with the others. But there are no boundaries to it. It never comes to an end.

Our act of living unites with another's act of living, and both go on to unite with a third, and so on. We make up a living net of radiant energies, each center indwelling every other center. All isolation, all loneliness, and all privacy are radically impossible on this level. In fact, they are meaningless. The whole of living reality is present in us and we in it. We cannot do anything on the excuse that it affects us alone and therefore is only our own business. We are always engaged in Reality's business. It is in this context that we live by creating the future.

The Future as Radical Novelty

The act of living is on the interface between the present and the future, not between the present and the past. Spondic energy is poured out toward the future. "To live" means "to create the future." When we love someone, for instance, we love that person as a "living one," one who has not yet existed but is just on the point of coming into existence, or we may say, one who is and who is coming to be. We pour energy into this nascent act of existing. Our intention is to contribute to the creation of this person.

The temptation is to think that the beloved person either exists or does not exist. We have images of persons coming into existence at the moment of conception or at some other definite time. We are accustomed to thinking of the people we had lunch with today as already existing, not in need of being created. This betrays our imaginations as still identifying the person with a description, an intersection of categories, an accumulation of past events. But as living ones these persons are being created from moment to moment. They are creating their own lives, our lives, and our common world. We also are creating their lives, our lives, and our common world.

Thus when we love someone, we do not love that person's past. The person to whom our agape love, our spondic energy, is directed is the person who does not yet quite exist, but who hovers on the horizon of the future. This person is in continuity with the one who presently exists and tends toward that future, and the present one is in continuity with the one of the past. But this is not to say that it is "the same" person.

How do we judge "sameness"? Do we not compare descriptions? If they match, we judge in favor of sameness; if they do not match, we declare for difference. But this method does not work in the case of our living personal beings. We want to claim that we are "the same" person all our life, yet we know that we are very different now in our descriptions from the way we were years ago. The unity of our personal being is not grounded in "sameness" but in *continuity* from moment to moment.

This continuity is a giving forward of the energy of life and selfhood from this moment to the next. It is essentially the giving of the energy of life itself, pure and transcendent, not limited to any set of descriptions. The unity is in the act itself, not in any comparison of the products of the act of living. Any two segments of biography will always register as "different" in some respects, as well as "same" in others, and so cannot be used to justify unity of the person. We ourselves, as living, are the unity. No matter how "different" might be the products we left behind, *we* would still be the thread of unity because we are the creator of these products of life, and the unity derives from our activity of creating, the *doing* of it, not the *having done* it.

It is often argued that we nevertheless bring our past with us. Sometimes it is said that our past tells us who we are. Or we want to preserve the goodness and the value in past deeds and experiences. But it is not our past that tells us who "we" are, except in the sense of providing a context for our "description." On the contrary, *we* tell our past what *it* is, because we are the ones who have made the past to be as it is. We as living are far greater than the past. Why should we want to cling to these goods we have accumulated in the past? Why should we look backward to find the origin of our life? Abraham is dead, and the prophets. A greater than Abraham is *here*. We, the living, contain all that the past is and more. The fountain of living water springs up out of our *heart*, from the very *center* of ourselves as living, that is, from the present moment just as it gives itself forward into the future.

This "giving forward" toward the future is the projection of spondic energy, is agape love as prevenient grace, is forgiveness, is an act of creative freedom. All of these mean radical novelty, an image of, or participation in, the divine act of creating out of nothing. It is not a matter of reshuffling the elements of the past. We should remember that we are attempting to describe here what is called mythically the Resurrection Life. The Resurrection is not a return to dealing with the events of the past, an effort to decide which of seven brothers you are now married to, since you had been married to each of them. To raise such questions or to be interested in such relations and ways of defining one's being betrays a complete failure to understand what the Resurrection is all about. The God of the Resurrection is the God of the living, not of the dead.

We must take care not to make of the Resurrection itself an event in the past, or even in the fantasized future, which is only the re-shuffled past. The Resurrection is the act of living. To be in the Resurrection means to identify oneself as the act of living in its creative continuity from moment to moment. The Resurrection is now and is ever moving. It cannot be clung to, for it is always ascending toward the future, the invisible, the unpredictable.

Genuine futurity is that which does not yet exist and therefore cannot be known. In relating ourselves to the future, we do not project ahead a goal or a target and then aim for it by selecting one course of action among several as that one most likely to enable us to reach the goal. That is prudent behavior when dealing with the predictable and is the operation of choice freedom. The creative freedom that characterizes the Resurrection Life does what seems a much smaller thing. It creates only the very next moment, exercising the continuity of the act of living as an artistic improvisation.

Probably we do not understand improvisation yet. Our ways of understanding have been by means of structures and other more or less fixed forms that belong essentially to the past. How *can* we understand radical novelty, that which is new all the way down to its root, not merely a development of something once given, but something that continues to be new again with each succeeding moment? How do we comprehend a self or a world or a Deity that says of each moment of its life, "Behold, I make all things new"? Creativity, as transcendently free improvisation of radical novelty, may have to become a whole new philosophical and theological topic, studied in its own terms.

Perhaps we may say that our positive energetic orientation toward the future is an act of faith precisely because the future cannot be known—or extrapolated or projected—but must be improvised. Having faith, in this context, means being willing that each moment should be new, radically new, unknown up to the time that it actually appears over the horizon of the future or takes shape as the dance of our creative energies.

The capacity to accept and deal with novelty is a mark of a higher type of life. The simpler life forms are the ones with more limited ranges of response, the ones that are preprogrammed to the few interactions with their environments that are necessary to enable them to continue. Their worlds are very repetitious. We ourselves still tend to be conservative in this regard, reluctant to expend our energy and jeopardize our accustomed sense of security by facing the world as constantly new. This spiritual sloth lures us into making stereotypes and formulating our lives along fixed tracks. The more we can assign life experiences to established categories, the easier we think life will be.

But growth in the spiritual order may be measured by willingness to let each being and each event be unique, willingness to accept creativity, willingness to see the world as new from moment to moment. If there is a gene in our hereditary make-up that promotes the advance of evolution by encouraging mutation and variability, the biologists say that it is a gene not for foreseeing the future but for nurturing the capacity for change.

We may ask, do all these changes ever achieve anything? Does this advancing evolution finally come to some culmination? Suppose our living core *is* the act of continuity of creating the self/world from moment to moment by our willingness to see it new, to admit its freshness, its uniqueness, its unknowability up to the moment of its appearance, and its unending novelty. Does this process never come to an end? Does it not sometime attain its goal?

What are we imagining when we ask these questions? Yes, I would say, life does attain its goal; it becomes what it is supposed to be, fulfills itself, precisely by never coming to an end. If it ever did come to an end in which there was no more novelty, there would be no more life; it would be dead. If the goal of our life is union with God, the archetypal Living One, and if the improvisation of continuous radical novelty is the characteristic of the Living One, then when we are united with God, we find our fulfillment by participating in this creative activity. And this fulfillment consists in continuing to create, world without end.

The Person as Process and Interpersonhood

I will repeat here something that I have said several times before in various places. We want the world to be a better place. We want the quality of life to be better. We want people to have good will toward one another and to behave respectfully and cooperatively. So we have devised ethical systems and we have preached a great deal about morality. We have found it necessary to back up our preaching with sanctions and the cultivation of guilt feelings. This method still does not work very well and we feel rather frustrated about the whole matter.

Why has our preaching and our punishing been so futile? My suggestion is that we have not had a metaphysics to sustain our morality. By metaphysics I means a spontaneous and natural worldview, the way we see reality without thinking about it, our taken-for-granted perception of being, or outlook on life. Our morality tells us to love others as ourselves. But our metaphysics says that others are alien to ourselves. Others are outside us, different, in competition with us, holding themselves in existence by repelling us, even as we must hold ourselves in existence by repulsing—or manipulating—them.

It is no use our saying poetically and sentimentally, "No man is an island." We believe in our bones that each of us *is* an island. All our cultural institutions—not excluding the institutional preachers themselves, the church and lawful civil society—are set up on this basis and encourage us by their very structure, as well as by their words, deeds, and omissions, to see the world in terms of separation, alienation, and domination. The result, of course, is that we experience a head-on internal conflict, and it is not to be wondered at that we feel confused and frustrated.

The metaphysics that will sustain the morality we preach, and the world we long for, is a metaphysics that genuinely perceives other persons as ourselves. The basic recommendation for the good life is not to love your neighbor *as much as* you love yourself, or even *in the same way as* you love yourself. It is to love your neighbor as *actually being* yourself. The fundamental *perception of selfhood* has to change before we can have the moral world we want.

I have tried, therefore, both to present a viable concept of the self as "the living one" and to stimulate or provoke some experience of it. The important thing is not so much that we should formulate a new *concept* of selfhood, although that must not be neglected, as that we should *perceive*—actually experience—selfhood in a new way. The new perception must become a natural, spontaneous, and inevitable, taken-for-granted, way of seeing the world before it can become the ground of our morality.

So we first must get away from the perception of the self as the personality, the description, and realize the self as transcendent. This enables us to experience ourselves as free, with creative freedom. Creative freedom improvises its self/world from moment to moment, always radically new. My contention is that the germ, the really vital part of ourselves, the quintessential "livingness" in us, lies right in this core of the transcendent self that is free, creative, and new from moment to moment. I am arguing that the *metanoia*, the shift in metaphysics that will give us the ground for the morality we desire—and consequently the life and the world that we desire—is a shift in our sense of where our selfhood is located, from the dead periphery of the personality description, to this living core of transcendent and creative freedom.

Now, initially this seems unreal, which is only to be expected if our sense of reality is not yet anchored there. We perceive our self as existing in space and in a spatialized time: the past and fantasized future that is structurally equivalent to the past. To think that our reality is concentrated in the fleeting instant that is the interface between the present and the future is to reduce ourselves from something substantial to something ephemeral. What I am proposing is that we simply invert this perception and regard this "instant"— the moment to moment continuity of living—as the primary reality, the substantial reality, and the spatialized past and pseudofuture as the secondary reality, shadowy and unsubstantial.

Thus the self, the person, is not the accumulation of the past, the spatialized substance that has some volume to it, some weight, but is the continuity, the creative activity of projecting life to the next instant. The person is not a product but is the process. Cut this process as fine as you like, the person is new in each such artificial frame. This is why it makes no sense to "forgive" your brother seven times; if you are to relate to your living brother at all, you must "forgive" him— give yourself intensively into his act of living—seventy times seven, that is, indefinitely, that is, from moment to moment, forever. The sense of time must become living, not spatialized and countable. Our living reality cannot be captured, enclosed, bounded, and defined. It is always moving.

Someone may ask, does not a person's identity or reality include the body? Is not the body spatial, enclosed, bounded, and defined? I propose this answer: The *personality's* body is defined and limited in this way, yes. But the *person's* true body is that greater reality that is called in the Christian tradition "the Mystical Body of Christ."

This Mystical Body is composed of a multitude of persons. They live in a shared Body by a shared Life. Each of them is a transcendent "I am" that is identically a spondic "May you be," radiating life and love, the energetic will for abundant being, to each of the others. Each is an agape lover and loves the lover in each other person. For in willing good and abundant life to another person, what can we will more than that this person should be a vital lover also? Thus each lover lives by spiritually indwelling each other lover; each person exercises personhood by uniting with each other person's personhood. Fundamental to personhood is that it is *interpersonhood*.

When we experience our selfhood this way, we will perceive all bodies as our body. We will say of everyone, "This at last is bone of my bones and flesh of my flesh." And we will confirm and celebrate a great marriage by saying, not alone "these two," but "these Many have become One Flesh." Would not this be the meaning of a universal Holy Communion, in which we each would give to every other our own life in the act of living, saying, "Take and eat, this is my body"? Mutually assimilating one another, we would unite our living processes and constitute a compound Person with this compound Mystical Body. Our shared and complex interpersonhood process would become the metaphysical ground that would naturally and inevitably sustain the attitude and behaviors that can create the world we desire.

The Holy Community

The Holy Communion exists to feed, to give life to, the Holy Community. It brings us to a dramatic and concrete experience of our processive interpersonhood as the revelation of the true root of our being. Whoever sees this full Person, the interpersonhood, sees the Origin of Life. This central insight, our argument claims, is that true life for a person is found in the living moment of creating the future, shared in the interpersonhood that is one's complete selfhood.

We may touch the central insight even more succinctly by referring once more to the mythic model of Holy Thursday and the prayer of Jesus that "they"—meaning us—"may be one, as we"—meaning the Persons of the Trinity—"are one." This saying should provoke us to ask, how are the Persons of the Trinity one? The Greek conception of the Trinity is very suggestive here. The Greek view emphasizes not so much the singular nature of the Godhead as the intercommunion of the living Persons. Each Person is described as so filled with the energy of self-giving to the others in outpouring love that a "reciprocal irruption," or unceasing circulation, of life results. This is the *peri-choresis* of the Trinity, whereby each Person indwells the others, and this interchange of love and life is what produces or constitutes the Divine Unity.

This is a most remarkable conception. It suggests something that we would not ordinarily affirm, namely that the Archetype of Being is a Community. Manyness is as real in the Ultimate Reality as is Unity. This is a difficult, and therefore an unpopular, notion for us. Who practices devotion to the Trinity the way people practice devotion to Jesus or Krishna or Kuan Yin? We are so accustomed to perceiving *ourselves* as simply unitary that we inevitably regard God as a single Person—something that the Preface in the liturgy of the Trinity in the Roman Missal, interestingly enough, expressly denies. But "manyness" in God sounds to us like polytheism, and we immediately reject it. What is hard for us to grasp is that the complex unity of the Trinity, fruit of their interpersonhood, is neither simple unity nor simple multiplicity. To be realized, it must be sought through our own experience of interpersonhood, arising from our own experience of the act of living.

The Preface of the Trinity can help us further by spelling out a few details, indicating "distinctness in Persons," "oneness in being," and "equality in majesty," all of which we can easily see to be explicitations of the nature of the Godhead, which is said by this same tradition to be agape. Only agape, of all relations, has this peculiar quality that it effects simultaneously a differentiation of the persons concerned, a union among them, and an acknowledgment of their equality in value.

If we reflect now on our contention that we are the image of God, we must conclude that we, also, are intended to be essentially a community, a holy community, established by agape, which effectively grounds our distinctness as persons, our oneness in being, and our equality in value. We, also, exist in a *perichoresis*, an unceasing circulation of life.

In this community, each one is precious, so that the community cannot afford to lose even one, and on the other hand, no one can experience the reality and fullness of life except through life in the community. No one can dominate another, or be of greater value than another, or in any way identify oneself by contrast with another. For the seeming "other" is not actually other at all, when we look more closely, but is our own self, an extension of our own mystical body. We cannot despise our own flesh, even in this extension, and we experience sensitively that whatever is done to anyone, is done to us. Our sense of being alive is extended universally as we realize that wherever two or three persons are gathered together in community, there we also are in the midst of them.

To sum up now, we can participate in the Holy Thursday revolution by shifting our perception of selfhood and our sense of reality from the dead descriptions of our past to the transcendent central selfhood that is continuously engaged in the act of living by the exercise of creative freedom, creating the future in radical novelty from moment to moment. Our personhood is revealed as a participation in this Resurrection Life and as an interpersonhood in which we pour forth energies of love into one another and thus organically unite ourselves into one Body, living by a shared and communicated life. We realize ourselves as a holy community in the image of the Trinity by acknowledging and practicing the *perichoresis*, the mutual indwelling, of the Divine Persons, and in this way we become, like them, a vital unity, a Living One.

NINE

Freedom

"If Anyone Is in Christ,
That Person Is a New Creation"

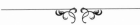

There is a basic urgency in life to grow, to expand, to become new and renewed. We might almost say that the very meaning of being alive is to be constantly in the process of becoming a new creation. This happens on small scales with every biological form we know, and it happens—or we can interpret our observations as if it were happening—on a large scale in the universe as a whole. At least one contemporary view of the cosmos sees it as one huge, dynamic, evolving being that passes through a series of stages in which its forms and internal relations assume ever new patterns.

Some theorists of evolution—notably Teilhard de Chardin—point out that with each succeeding stage of development the complexity of the patterns is increased. So also are the unity of the form, the differentiation of the composing elements, and the "interiority"—or "subjectivity," or "consciousness," or "freedom"—of the new being. As more complex creatures are formed by the union of less complex elements, the range and variety of the creatures' activities are extended, the integration of their various faculties and operations is improved, and their capacity to respond to the presence of alternative possibilities is increased. Consequently, the ability of successive creatures to focus their behavior is heightened, and the precursor forms of purpose and self-possession appear.

Eventually, a critical threshold is reached, and the expanding, complexifying, intensifying, unifying interiority, or consciousness, becomes *reflexive:* conscious of being conscious. Beyond this point, the speculative theorist of evolution may propose that the general urgency toward growth and renewal that characterizes the universe as a whole seems—in our local neighborhood—to concentrate its energy and focus its best efforts on further evolution of this reflexive consciousness. Perhaps the significant mutations now are not to be expected in anatomical and physiological patterns but in patterns of thinking, knowing, feeling, desiring, choosing, willing.

Precisely at this point a curious situation can arise. With the appearance of reflexive consciousness, freedom attains the form that we usually consider normative, the ability to make deliberate choices among alternative courses of action. Now, the evolution theorist suggests, we may look for a mutation in this reflexive consciousness, in this free consciousness, in this *reflexively free* consciousness—this consciousness that freely chooses the ways in which it will use its freedom. However, if this reflexively free consciousness is to undergo mutation, and if the mutation is to consist of changes in the way this consciousness freely operates, then the mutation can take place only if it is freely chosen by the reflexive consciousness itself.

All the urgency toward growth and renewal that is the essence of life, all the pressure of a dynamic universe to expand and increase its being, come to a crossroads—and may come to a dead halt—in this involuted being, the reflexively conscious, reflexively free, creature.

It is against this cosmic backdrop of a possible universal evolution toward ever new creation that I wish to discuss the topic of this chapter: What is the mutation in our free consciousness that must take place in order to produce the new creation that is characterized by being "in Christ"? And how will the character of this new creation give us one more answer to the question, "Who do people say I am?"

I am going to describe a certain kind of mutation in consciousness that seems to me to be both desirable in its own right and called for as the next logical step in the evolution of the universe as outlined in the brief sketch just given. I am also going to suggest that this particular mutation in consciousness, or *metanoia,* can be viewed as the movement of our freedom that gives rise to the new creation that is "in Christ." In order to illustrate this mutation dramatically, I will utilize a scriptural story, interpreting it with a mythmaker's license to encapsulate the meaningful comments on human life that I myself wish to make.

The mutation in consciousness that I believe we are called to make at this stage in our evolution is a shift from what I have called the *domination paradigm* of human relations to what I have called the *communion paradigm.* I will analyze these paradigms in detail, speaking of the metaphysics and the logic implied, of something I call the "physics" of the paradigms, because it has to do with energy relations, and of the psychology involved. In the course of doing this, I will treat the meaning and role of freedom; my interpretation of the words "in Christ" will emerge, and major emphasis will be given to a discussion of the "new creation." But first, let us look at a dramatic illustration of the mutation in consciousness that takes place when a community shifts from the domination paradigm to the communion paradigm.

The Holy Thursday Revolution

The scene is the Cenacle; the occasion, the last supper that Jesus shares with his disciples. There are two main events, the first representing the destruction of the old paradigm, the second representing the institution of the new.

Jesus begins his destructive and creative action by washing the feet of his companions. This is a menial task ordinarily performed by a servant. For Jesus, the master, to execute this function is a shocking reversal of the proper roles of the Rabbi and his disciples, or servants. What makes it so shocking is that it concretizes an inversion of the *social* relations that themselves reflect what we may call the *metaphysical* relations of the beings involved.

In a world structured by the domination, or lordship, paradigm, footwashing is a nonreciprocal relation. Servants wash the feet of their lords. Lords do not wash the feet of their servants. Epitomized in this homely gesture are all the nonreciprocal relations of domination that are the structural principles of a whole world of human and divine/human relations.

The depth of investment that the human race has made in the domination paradigm is represented by the vehemence with which Peter resists the reversal into which Jesus has plunged them. "Lord!" he exclaims—reminding Jesus of the role he is expected to maintain—"you shall never wash my feet!" But Jesus cannot be forced back into a social and metaphysical position he is determined to destroy. He warns Peter that unless Peter consents to this destruction of his former sense of how the world is patterned, he cannot enter into the new life that Jesus wishes to share with him.

As a paradigm, this sense of the world's structure has not been directly perceived: rather, everything else has been perceived in its terms, fitted to the categories and the models that it has made psychologically and culturally available. Only when Jesus inverts the social gesture, and thereby inverts the metaphysical relation, does the nature of the paradigm itself rise to clear consciousness.

Jesus spells it out plainly: "Do you realize what I have done? If we use the paradigm of lord and servants, then I must be the lord, while you are the servants. But here I have given you an example of my conception of our true relationship. The one who is supposed to be the lord has washed the feet of those who are supposed to be the servants. But I have not acted out of condescension. You will miss my point completely if you are merely overwhelmed that the Lord has so lowered himself as to wash your feet. That would change nothing, fundamentally, and my intention is to transform radically your whole world. By this act I mean to declare that I do not accept the relationship of lord and servants at all. I will no longer call you servants, but friends."

Thus does the old paradigm of domination as the structural principle of human relations perish. A whole order of the world dies here on the cross of contradiction by Jesus' free act of refusing to see things in that way.

A new world rises to replace it, as Jesus institutes a new model of human and of divine/human relations in the second great event of this evening, the Holy Communion. Choosing a fitting medium for this concretization of his vision and his free intention, Jesus shares his own life substance and life energy with his friends under the guise of food. He wishes them to have life and to have it more abundantly, and to this end he gives himself as nourishment into their lives. This is his love for them. As he has done, so they are to do: "Love one another as I have loved you. Give your life substance and your life energy into the lives of each other. Become nourishment for one another that life may become more abundant among all of you."

Jesus has created a new set of personal-relation dynamics, reflecting his own insight into the metaphysical structure of things, which he explains by saying: "I am in you, and you are in me"—the model of human relations—and "I am in God, and God is in me"—the model of divine/human relations. He adds another image: "I see myself as a vine, of which all of you are the branches. You are part of my very being, as I am of yours. Together we form a single living being, a growing, climbing, fruit-bearing being."

The great work comes to its completion; the fullness of the revelation is made: all that Jesus has learned of Reality he has now made known. It remains for his friends to assimilate the vision, to realize its implications, to appreciate how different this communion paradigm is from the domination paradigm of the world, and to work out how they may put it into practice without succumbing to the temptation to make compromises with the old way.

This is my mythic presentation of the contrasting paradigms and of the mutation in consciousness that I believe is our passage into the new creation. Now let us analyze them.

The Domination Paradigm

The domination paradigm of social relations has a long evolutionary history. There is no need to describe it at length, for it is obvious all around us, in birds' pecking orders, dominance relations among primates, and in the social (by sex, race, class), economic, and political structures of our own civilizations. It has given life good service, enabling it to survive and spread. If we now suggest that we are facing the possibility of a free mutation from this paradigm to another, the reason must be that the urgency in life to become new again and to achieve a more complex unity requires it.

The expansion and reflexivity of human consciousness itself will lead to this question of the mutation. Perhaps we are now ready to live according to a principle other than that which serves life in these lower orders. In this context we might even recast traditional language and say that, relative to the community organizing principle of those social animals (including ourselves) that nature has so far produced, the new principle that will give form to a new creation can be called "supernatural."

Domination is a nonreciprocal relation of determination of being: of the fact that a being is, or of what it is, or of how it can act, or of how it is to be valued. The dominator determines the being of the dominated in a way that the dominated does not, perhaps cannot, determine the being of the dominator. This gives us, on the social level, our familiar authority and power structures, with their emotional auras of respect, or reverence, or fear, and not infrequently of hostility. It produces one kind of unity, under a single authority, and thus makes possible concerted action, which has definite advantages for life.

The unity under authority and power is, of course, an imposed unity, *extrinsic* to the beings unified by it. The beings themselves are separate entities. In fact, their separation and their *alienation* from one another are necessary presuppositions for this type of unity. Each being is "other" to every being in the collectivity so gathered. Each is "outside" every other and must be related to the others by some external relation that produces a forced unity among the elements.

The energy that produces the *unity* and the energy that maintains the *separate entity* that is a member of the unity are different and conflicting energies. The individual entity aims to maintain itself in terms of its own natural unity, and the collectivity aims to produce itself by the imposition of artificial external relations originating in the determinative actions of the dominating authority. The two energies, or forces, are held in tension, in some degree of balance, because the domination paradigm is dependent on both of them being operative.

Domination, because it is a nonreciprocal relation, can operate only between beings that are quite separate and outside one another, so the separation and exteriority must be maintained. But domination, by determining the beings of the dominated, also produces unity. The separation and the unity are two sides of one paradigm of social relations.

We experience this tension and conflict in what we call the problem of the individual and the community, and we puzzle over how much value to give each side and how to reconcile them. The unity of the community is always difficult to achieve because the psychological forces that keep the separation in place are dynamically opposed to it.

In order to have separate beings that are mutually "other," each being must have some characteristics that the other beings do *not* have. Its claim to selfhood, in this paradigm, is based on *negating* the attributes of others—or, in a social context, negating their actions or negating their value. Each being in a domination paradigm has to say "I am I insofar as I am not-you," and "You are you insofar as you are not-I." It is easy enough to see that in a social context of activities and values the "I am I" will often be secured by making sure of the "You are not-I," that is, by depriving others of certain attributes, activities, or values that then become the exclusive property of the "I."

I call this the logic of self-identification by *mutual negation*. It underlies the metaphysics of *alienation,* or dependence of being on "otherness," which in turn is the foundation for the social relations of domination and the psychological experiences associated with the perception of inferiors and superiors.

The Communion Paradigm

Does the communion paradigm offer any alternative to this deep structure? It is my contention that it does, that the difference between domination and communion is not merely a matter of moral attitudes in which sympathy and generosity replace pride and selfishness. I argue that we cannot effectively change our behavior in the moral context until we have first somehow performed a gestalt shift in our perceptions of how being is basically constituted.

To urge people to love one another as they love themselves, while simultaneously reinforcing them by every aspect of our culture, including our religious institutions, in their perception of their world as structured by a logic of mutual negation and a metaphysics of alienation, is to generate a direct, and inevitably painful, conflict. And to make a mystique of the suffering entailed in trying to live with this conflict is only to hide from ourselves what is really causing the trouble.

The communion paradigm, as presented in my mythic version of Holy Thursday, is a reciprocal relation of the enhancement of being. This is in contrast to the domination paradigm, which, I said, is a nonreciprocal relation of the determination of being. "I am in you" and "You are in me" read the same in both directions. Unlike the domination paradigm in which the elements are outside one another, the communion paradigm sees beings as *in* one another.

What does this mean? It is difficult for us to say, because all the rest of our experience is made up of perceptions of things that are seen as outside one another. When I come to the discussion of the "physics" of this new way of being, I will try to describe this being "in" at great length, but now I will only point out the contrasts that parallel what was said about the domination paradigm.

Being "outside" meant being "other," or "alien," by having attributes, activities, or values that were *denied* to the beings one was outside or other than. To be "in" a fellow being must then mean that instead of denying one's attributes, activities, and values to one's fellow, one *gives* them, somehow *puts them into* the fellow being. This is what the story says Jesus did by putting himself, under the guise of food, literally *into* his companions. His substance and energy, his attributes, activities, and values are assimilated by them and live in them as their own attributes, activities, and values. Jesus says as much: "Whoever receives you, receives me"; "Whatever anyone does to my brother or sister, is done to me"; "The works I have done you shall do also"; "God loves you as God loves me"; and so on.

This reciprocal relation of communion and being "in" one another produces unity, as the domination relation did, but a very different kind of unity. The unity under the dominating authority was imposed from the outside and remained extrinsic to the beings unified. The unity attained by communion arises from the very interiority of the beings united, from their presence in the midst of each other, and it must be freely accepted. Jesus had to obtain Peter's consent to the paradigm shift before it could take place. And each one who received the life of Jesus as nourishment had freely and deliberately to eat it. Consequently, the union so obtained is an *intrinsic* union: the very core of each person's being, each one's freedom, has enacted the giving and receiving that constitute the union.

This communion unity also contrasts with the unity under domination by not being based on conflicting energies, one to maintain the individual member in separateness and another to maintain the concerted behavior of the community. In the community united by the communion paradigm, the same energy simultaneously establishes the self-being of the composing members and the union among them. The members see themselves, not as *possessors* of exclusively claimed attributes, but as *acts* of giving themselves to their fellows. This way of identifying themselves is part of the paradigm of their perception of being in general. Thus, they experience their love for one another as simultaneously establishing themselves in being and establishing their union.

But what, we may want to ask, distinguishes them from one another if not the fact that each has certain attributes that the others do not have? Is not all determination founded on negation? No doubt, but need all self-identity be a matter of "de-*term*-ination," a matter of setting *terms*, that is, ends, to being? In the communion paradigm, in which one says "I am I insofar as I am in you," rather than "I am I insofar as I am not-you," there is no way of setting terminations to one's being. One gives oneself into a fellow being, there to live in and with a further life. But then that fellow being also is engaged in sharing life energy with further companions, and so one's life is carried along in the current of life energy passed from friend to friend without any particular limit being given. So, there are two ways that limitation, which could be used to define and secure one's sense of identity, is not used: it is not used to limit the *kind* of being one has by negating the kind of being another has, and it is not used to set bounds to the "extent" of one's being by circumscribing even the sharing one does.

To people reared in the metaphysics of alienation, where being is established by determination, by fixing the borders, the boundaries of being by negation, this must sound vague, indefinite, unsubstantial, and insecure. "What will happen to my identity in this communion paradigm?" they ask uneasily.

Jesus says that if we try to preserve our lives, we will lose them, but that if we are willing to give our lives into him and his community in accordance with the new vision he is presenting, then we shall live without limit. The seeking to preserve one's life is the attempt to protect what one possesses of being by denying one's own life to others. This method, while it works for the definition of objects in the world—including people, insofar as they are considered "objects," thrown outside one another—is precisely wrong for persons and must come to a self-destructive end when applied to them. It does not see deeply enough into the nature of the evolving reflexively conscious being. It does not leave enough room for expansion and growth, and especially, it does not provide an opening for the mutation in consciousness that enables life to renew itself.

On the other hand, if we identify ourselves as acts of life enhancement by sharing our lives with our fellows, then life can go on indefinitely, growing, expanding, complexifying and unifying, rising to new levels of consciousness and freedom. The question for us is, can we feel secure living without limits, without negations? What can we put in their place to establish our self-identity?

Just as the domination paradigm is built on a metaphysics of alienation, rooted in a logic of self-identity by mutual negation, so is the communion paradigm built on a metaphysics of indwelling, rooted in a logic of self-identity by *mutual affirmation*. The secret of self-identity does not lie in an external setting of boundaries to being by negation and separation, but in an internal coincidence with the act of living itself. To live is to communicate life, because life is essentially a spreading, growing phenomenon. Therefore, the more one communicates life, affirms life in one's fellows, gives oneself to enhance their lives, the more one is alive, is truly living, and thus is truly oneself.

To see self-identity as founded by negation is to look at beings from the outside, to look at their shells as it were, the dead cuticles of their beings. Jesus is trying to get people to see how the world they have been believing in, valuing, and acting in terms of, is a *dead* world, a world of outsidedness, of negation, of boundaries and separations. "Let the dead bury their dead," he says, and you come with me into life by realizing your self-identity in your living acts of *affirming* your fellow beings, experiencing yourself as living in your companions, not outside them.

Evolution has produced reflexive consciousness: consciousness of consciousness, and consciousness of freedom. Consciousness of ourselves from the outside was only a first stage of this reflexivity. We might describe it as a consciousness *that* we are conscious beings. And the first stage of freedom was to choose among various external actions. But the evolutionary pressure toward greater reflexivity urges us to a realization of ourselves as conscious *of* being conscious, a noetic coincidence with ourselves as conscious acts of life-communicating life. This noetic coincidence with the act of communicating life is itself a free act; it is now a our *interior* act that nevertheless enters more profoundly into the interiority of our *fellow* beings than ever an external act touched the exteriority of an *other* being.

In the communion paradigm we would say that self-identity is rooted in reflexivity, in interior coincidence with the unlimited activity of living itself, not in determination by negation.

I said that it is the general urgency in life toward realizing itself as an ever new creation that somehow propels us to the threshold of the mutation in consciousness by which we enter "into Christ" and into the communion paradigm of conscious relations. But, I also said, this mutation is unlike any mutation evolutionary nature has ever before experienced, because this one must be freely performed by the mutants themselves. I want now to say a few words about freedom in the context of transcendence and the reflexivity I have just mentioned. The understanding of freedom as emerging from the transcendence that reflexivity makes possible is important as a preparation for what will be said about energy relations in the new creation in Christ.

Reflexivity and Transcendence

I want to emphasize that this mutation is to be based on an intensification of the reflexivity of consciousness, because some systems of spirituality that have mystical union with God as their goal teach that reflexive consciousness is an impediment to this union. They intend, as I also intend, to shift from a consciousness of separation and alienation to a consciousness of union, but they believe that in order to do that we must give up, or overcome, that doubling of consciousness whereby we are aware of ourselves doing whatever we are doing interiorly. So long as we admit such a duality of consciousness, we have not attained perfect union with the Absolute Being.

Other schools of spirituality are alarmed by this teaching and point out that abandonment of all duality would mean the loss of everything that we are as unique, individual, human persons. These schools usually feel that individual selfhood can be secured only by the negation/determination method. Both they and the nondualists seem to have in mind the duality established by objectification, by consciousness *that* we are operating as a conscious being that can be identified by its difference from other beings and, in particular, by its distinction from the object of its consciousness.

What I want to suggest is that there is a third way. The negation/determination method should not be used to identify persons, but neither should personal identity and its reflexive consciousness be totally abandoned. It is not the *reflexivity* as such that interferes with union, either with God or with fellow human persons, but the *type* of reflexivity and the *identification* of that reflexive consciousness—the definition and localization of it—by means of negation, alienation, and objectification. We need only change the type of reflexivity and the method by which the reflexive consciousness is identified in order to make the reflexivity a positive, indeed a necessary, condition for entering into union, rather than an impediment to it.

The communion consciousness that I am proposing as a desirable next phase in our evolution and as a new creation in Christ is not a loss of all self-consciousness in some kind of undifferentiated mass consciousness in which all become simply and unqualifiedly one. It is rather a radical break with one way of doing self-consciousness and the adoption of another way of doing self-consciousness. I say "doing self-consciousness," rather than "being self-conscious," in order to underline the reflexivity and the freedom: our self-consciousness is not simply there, but we *perform it* as an act of living, and we may perform it in one way in preference to another.

The first stage of reflexive consciousness, I said, was consciousness *that* we are conscious beings. This is imperfect reflexivity because
it separates the subject who is "conscious that" from the object who is
a "conscious being." This "conscious being," which, like any object,
has to be categorized and indexed in order to be known, we may call
an *individual*. This is to distinguish the kind of entity identified by this
method from the kind identified by the second stage of reflexivity,
which we may call a *person*. This is a worthwhile distinction to make,
because it corresponds to the distinction between the domination
paradigm, with its logic of negation, and the communion paradigm,
with its logic of affirmation, and enables us to say that only persons
can enter into communion consciousness. Individuals remain external to one another.

The kind of self-identity and reflexivity that are practiced by
being conscious of what we are as *individuals* is an exercise in *abstract
intelligence*. We enumerate all the categories that seem appropriate to
ourselves, and then recognize ourselves as individual instances of
these classes. If we are to identify ourselves by this type of description
and seek to justify our uniqueness in such terms, we will have to pile
up more and more predicates, hoping thereby to so limit the class to
which we belong that it will contain only one member. But, all these
abstractions will not catch the true self that we are as a concrete
being, and we will probably have the insight to realize this. We will
feel that our "I" is somehow more than all these descriptions and that
it would still be itself, even if the description changed.

To realize our self as *person*, we must begin with the concrete
being and never leave the concrete being that is our self as actually
existing. To know our self as a concrete act of existence, we must give
up identifying our self in terms of abstractions. We need to develop a
concrete intelligence.

We can usefully identify objects abstractly, but if we would know
our self, we must remember that it is a subject and, therefore, must be
approached by a different method. We cannot *look at* or *talk about* a
subject. To do so is to convert it into an object. We must rather *noetically coincide with* our self by experiencing our own existence interiorly. This is what I called the second stage of reflexivity, and this time
it is a perfect reflexivity, because it does not make the subject into an

object but knows the subject precisely as a subject. Thus, it does not produce duality.

How, exactly, do we go about "noetically coinciding with" our self as subject? I suggest a meditation exercise. Say to yourself, "I am such-and-such," filling in the "such-and-such" with whatever predicates are appropriate in your case. Make some of the predicates simple physical qualities, such as height or weight or gender, others biographical and concerned with social relations, such as being so-and-so's son or daughter or spouse, or being a member of a certain society or church or nation. Finally, make some of the predicates personality attributes and qualities of intelligence and character. This is our familiar way of sensing ourselves, so there is no particular difficulty in doing it.

Now, existentially center yourself in the experience of being "I am such-and-such." Concretely feel yourself as such a being. Identify with existing in this way. Next, begin to experiment with varying the predicates with which you identified yourself. If you said "I am short," say "I am tall," and so on. Discover that the concrete sense "I am" remains stable despite these changes. Go beyond merely altering the predicates; remove them altogether, beginning with the physical ones and working gradually toward the more interior ones. Take care to remain actively, presently, concretely centered in the sense "I am" as you do this.

This stripping of yourself of the predicates will give you a vivid realization of the distinction between the predicates as abstract categories and your existential self as a real concrete being. As the limitations represented by the objectifying abstract predicates are removed, the concrete subjective experience "I am" will expand. It will find itself freer and larger as it is less and less bound to this or that particular way of being. When all the predicates have been removed, the sense of identity will be profoundly centered in the act "I am" alone and will be immediately aware of itself as intrinsically living and luminous.

This self, which is our spiritual "protoplasm," so to speak, the very stuff of life, is thus transcendent of all the categories in which it can manifest itself. It *does* manifest itself through them; it does extend its identity to the descriptions in which it clothes itself in time and space. But, it is not bound by them. It gives its name to them; they do not give their name to the self.

It is this transcendence of the person over the individual that makes possible the communion consciousness of the new creation in Christ. The reason for this is that each level of new creation is, in general, produced by bonding the central energies of the unities of the preceding level. I will have more to say about this when we come to the energy relations, but the point here is that the central energies that we *persons* will bond to form the new creation in Christ are our *free* energies, and the free energies arise only on the level of our *transcendent* personhood.

A lot of mischief is done by trying to form communion on the level where we still identify ourselves in terms of categories—the qualities and attributes by which we describe ourselves to ourselves and distinguish ourselves from others. This produces conflict, as I explained earlier, because the energy of identity and the energy of attempted communion are working against each other. And the conflict produces guilt and any number of other miseries.

The pseudounions formed in these attempts are not true unions of the next higher order of complexity but only transient collectivities on this same level where we now exist. For instance, attractions between people that are based only on physical and emotional characteristics are highly unstable and have a high rate of dissolution. On the larger scale, totalitarian political regimes that impose artificial unity on a people usually end in disaster and disintegration. Unfortunately, such disintegrations are always followed by renewed attempts at artificial unity.

This is the reason it is essential to undergo a mutation of consciousness at a sufficiently deep level of our perceptions of ourselves and one another. As long as we identify ourselves and one another by our outside categories, by our "morphic descriptions," we produce only external and artificial unions; we cannot bond ourselves to one another in the heart of our beings, cannot reach a *personal* unity, which will be both a new level reality and a lasting one. We need to become "metamorphic," transcendent of all the forms that might limit us in their abstract categories, and to identify concretely with the sheer living reality of our personal selfhood as intensely reflexive consciousness and freedom.

Transcendent Freedom

We usually consider the normative form of freedom to be the ability to make deliberate choices among alternative courses of action. This kind of freedom can be exercised within the conception of ourselves according to abstract categories, within the domination paradigm, within the logic of negation and the metaphysics of alienation. What I want to suggest is that by deepening our sense of self-hood as reflexive consciousnesses to the point where we realize our transcendence of the categories and become "metamorphic," we touch another level of freedom. This freedom, which arises on the level of our transcendent selfhood, is not characterized so much by making choices among alternatives as by being an original source of action.

I have called the first type of freedom "choice freedom." In choice freedom, the action does not originate directly with the free agent but remotely somewhere amongst the various contingencies of the situation and in the complex interactions between the agent and the environment that eventually produce the alternatives that present themselves for choice. Only when the alternatives are recognized by the agent as presenting themselves for choice is there a call for action. At this point it seems that the action originates with the alternatives in the sense that *they* stimulate the agent to make the choice. The whole act of making a deliberate choice thus has a quality of "dependent origination" in that it is provoked or stimulated by the presentation of alternative courses and is limited by the field of alternatives presented.

The second type of freedom is "transcendent freedom." This is the freedom that arises on the metamorphic level, the level that I call personal, as distinguished from the level of the individual. The important point about transcendent freedom is that it has a quality of "independent origination." By that I mean that whether or not there are alternatives to the act undertaken, the act is free in the sense that it arises directly out of the initiative of the agent. It is not undertaken because it is stimulated by the presence of something calling for action; it is not a response to some quality in the environment. It is an original act that begins with the agent and has no antecedents outside the agent. Even in a case where there is no alternative to the action undertaken, the agent acts freely by acting out of a self-originated stimulation to act.

But, then, someone might say, there is at least the choice between acting or not acting at all. What I wish to say—and it is difficult to say this correctly—is that even in the case where there is no choice between acting and not acting, because the agent does act, even then the act is free when the energy for it arises immediately from the reflexive consciousness of the agent's transcendent personhood.

I think that we make a false problem for ourselves when we argue that the agent in such a case is "necessitated" by its own "nature." So the "nature" of a free agent is to be free. When it acts freely, is it then "necessitated" because its "nature" obliges it to act freely? I think this sort of reasoning does not really help us understand ourselves or help us advance to more desirable states of consciousness.

This is the reason concrete intelligence that produces concrete existential knowledge of oneself as a transcendent personal being is important. Abstract intelligence leads us into quibbles over concepts framed as paradoxical questions, but concrete intelligence gives us insight into what we are really trying to understand. The experienced sense of self as transcendent of our categories is for this reason an indispensable prerequisite to an appreciation of the sense in which we can act freely, whether or not there are alternatives present, provided the action arises immediately from our transcendent self as from its first source.

Does this mean, then, that the action arises originally and immediately from our own separate, finite, human being? No, that would be to describe it in terms of the old paradigm of the logic of negation and the metaphysics of alienation. Here we can make use of that other dimension of Jesus' revelation in the Holy Communion. We have developed the implications of his saying, "I am in you, and you are in me." Now we can turn to the parallel saying, "I am in God, and God is in me."

I apply this to each of us, and I say it is said of the transcendent personal being, the metamorphic being. Therefore, there is a sense in which we must say that the energy and the movement of the free act originates in God. Nevertheless, we must avoid following up this statement by saying, "It does not originate in us." We must also avoid thinking of God as outside us, separate from us, and ourselves as outside and separate from God. The metaphysics of mutual indwelling outlaws this. It would be a false problem and a throwback to the logic of negation to ask, "Is the energy to originate free acts God's or mine?" The energy of free action is both God's and mine. It originates in that center of interiority where the "in" by which God is *in me* and the "in" by which I am *in God* meet.

At first hearing, this may sound absurd or meaningless. We must take into consideration the fact that we have no fit language for this new paradigm of communion consciousness, this metaphysics of mutual indwelling. All our language has been designed to deal with beings that are outside one another. Statements which intend to undercut and reject the very foundations of this outsiders' language are therefore bound to sound absurd in that language. So, we are forced to say strange sounding things as invitations to experience with concrete intelligence the relations to which our attention is now being directed.

We have to keep remembering, as this exposition develops, that "I" *am* "I," not by virtue of being *not* some other being—even God— but precisely by virtue of being *in* other beings, preeminently God. My very "I-ness" consists in this being *in*. That is what the metaphysics of indwelling means.

Freedom on the personal, transcendent level, then, freedom that arises immediately and directly from the agent without provocation by the environment, is freedom that originates in the mutual interiority of God and the person. Realization of oneself as this kind of free agent is the necessary and proximate preparation for those energetic acts that will bond the free agents into a community "in Christ" and produce the new creation.

The Energy Relations

We come now to the discussion of what I called the "physics" of this new paradigm for social being. I call it "physics" because the relations that we bear to one another in the communion paradigm are more than just moral relations. They are real relations of real, concrete beings, and I find the metaphor of energy the most nearly satisfactory image for discussing this matter. Probably I should say that by "physics" I mean to include biology, using "physics" in the very old-fashioned sense to mean any and all natural relations and functions. Certainly, biological metaphors are most descriptive of the relations and processes I am trying to describe.

For instance, Jesus' act of giving himself as *food* to his friends is a vivid metaphor in the biological order of the real relationship of mutual indwelling in the personal order that it represents. At what point does food stop being "food" and become the one who has eaten it? Of course, the "food" in this case represents a being who is essentially alive and remains alive and self-identified after being "eaten." It is this metaphor of feeding that makes us realize the significance of the fact. Such a gesture is intended to point to the complex *organic* relationship among Jesus and his friends that is the foundation of being in the new creation. The sense in which Jesus lives in the person whom he feeds with his own life is not just an attitude of sympathy, alliance, and loyalty on his part or the other person's. It is a real way of being for both of them. What is at issue is not just a morality but a biology, or a physics if you will, of personal being.

So, I will describe the transcendent personal being, the being who is able to place the free act that will generate the new creation, in greater detail now under the imagery of energy and with physical and biological metaphors. Follow the description from inside a sense of concrete existential identification with your transcendent self, as gained from the meditation exercise suggested above (pp. 50–51).

When we do center ourselves in the concrete existential experience "I am," we realize that it is intrinsically living and luminous. By "luminous" I mean that it shines by light originating in its own interior, as distinguished from reflecting energy that originates outside.

This is that freedom of "independent origination" that is not a response to the environment but a spontaneous and self-initiated act. This is the transcendent self that is above and beyond all the abstract categories and predicates that would catch us in their limiting forms. As the metamorphic being, it may be experienced as a "still point" at the heart of our dance of manifestation in the finite world.

We no sooner touch this "still point" at the core of our being, this immutable at the heart of mutability, than we discover it as an explosion of energy. Our "I am" is simultaneously a "May you be," also. We find that the energy of existence that we are is intrinsically a radiant energy. It streams out from us in every way. It seems to be the nature of that which is "I am" to say "Let it be." This is what we might expect, since our free, luminous energy originates in the common point of our mutual interiority with the creative God, with the One whose proper name is I AM and whose characteristic utterance as Creator is *Fiat*, "Let it be."

I believe that if you will attend carefully to your own interior, you will actually experience this luminosity, this radiant spondic energy that rises up "like a spring in the heart, springing up unto unlimited life," unto the communication of life, the giving of abundant life.

It is an outpouring that we experience as a projection of personal, spiritual, self-existence energy toward and into other persons, and even toward the infrapersonal universe. We will to pour our own life, our own existence, into others, that they may be and may be abundantly. It is our own act, performed on our own initiative. It is not compelled, not automatic, not unconscious. It is the proper, or characteristic, act of a *person*. To share self-being with another in this central way is precisely what it means to be a person.

Our affirmation, therefore, is directed from our central self, transcendent and spondic, toward the other's central self, transcendent and spondic. We are in living contact with another "I am," a subjective existence. Both are beings jetting into the future, unknown from one instant to the next, improvising life as a free creation. Our spondic energy is poured toward the future, for the good of the future. It is not a reaction to the past, but a free promise to the world to come, where all things are still possible.

Unbounded Selfhood: Communion and Perichoresis

Continuing to pour energy of life and of goodness toward all, we not only do the most powerful thing that can be done to encourage good acts hereafter, but we loosen the hold of false identifications of our self and the other, and we deepen our realization of both of us as transcendent centers of spondic energy capable of communion.

Those into whom we pour our life are equally concrete, are existent persons, not "humanity at large." Each person is of such a nature that, if we give up identifying ourselves with the individual ego and coincide with ourselves as outflowing energy, we will discover that we can freely and consciously indwell every other person, and that every other person indwells us. Our whole sense of the "location" of our selfhood has to be reordered. This is the reason this new consciousness is a revolution.

By practicing noetic coincidence with our inmost transcendent self, and by following it in its outpouring movement, we find that "we" are actually living in the hearts, that is, in the central beings, of other persons. The other persons, moreover, are also fountains of spondic energy, pouring out to all beings. We are living in them, but they in turn are living in still others. The energy goes round in continual circulation, and each participant can truly claim to be "in" each of the others, to be "one" with each of the others, and with the whole radiant interaction.

This is the experience on the level of transcendent personal selfhood of the Holy Communion, a "union together" that composes a "whole" in the "sanctity" of mutual self-donation. The Holy Communion in turn can be seen in likeness to that other great metaphor of essential being proposed in the Christian tradition, the *perichoresis* of the trinitarian Godhead.

The three divine Persons are portrayed as so eagerly giving themselves to one another that their acts of life-exchange set up an unceasing circulation of self-energy that constitutes their unity in one being. This is the *perichoresis*, or *circumincession*, of the Persons of the Trinity, whereby they live and dwell in one another, where each is, not a static being, but a living process of further life-donation.

It is a life movement that perpetually communicates life, without beginning, without end. Since each Person becomes most truly the self that that Person is by performing this characteristic act of giving self-life to the other Persons, the spondic act of self-donation has the unique property of creating simultaneously both unity and differentiation. This is precisely what we need metaphysically as the foundation of being and, especially, as the foundation of our being as persons in relation to one another.

So if we ask, "What is the paradigm of being?" "What is God?" we may answer, "God is *perichoresis*; God is the mutual exchange of free spondic energies; God is love."

The New Creation

We are now in a position to pull all of this together and declare, *This* is the New Creation. I want to say three principal things about the New Creation: (1) that it is the next step in our evolution; (2) that it is an image of the Trinity; and (3) that it is aptly described by a phrase lifted from Scripture, in which Christ is called by the Angel of the Resurrection the "Living One," who is not to be sought among the dead.

Everything that I have said up to now has been said from the point of view of what each person must do in order to enter into Christ and into the New Creation. Now, I want to emphasize that the coming to be of the New Creation is a community event. Besides saying "If any *one* is in Christ, that person is a new creation," we must say, "If *we* are in Christ, *our community* is a new creation." And, of course, as I have defined "person," the first statement cannot exist without the second, for a person is precisely an energy radiating out to fellow persons in the community. The community is the interlocking affirming energies of all the persons of which it is composed.

The first thing I want to say about the new creation, then, is that it is a community, a compound unity composed of persons, each of whom is "in Christ," and all of whom together constitute the Body of Christ. As a compound unity, it can be seen as the next step in the cosmic pattern of evolution that I proposed in the beginning. Each level of relatively new creation up to reflexive consciousness has been formed by the union of lower level entities: atoms of the subatomic particles, molecules of atoms, cells of molecules, organisms of cells. Each time a new creature has been formed by such a union, the union has taken place dynamically by the exchange of the characteristic energies of the lower level entities. It is *energy sharing* that is the bonding, the union that makes the new level creature.

This is the reason it is important to discuss our being "in Christ" in terms of energy relations and energy sharing—the reason it is important is to distinguish the particular type of energy that is to be shared; namely, the energy of the transcendent personal center, the spondic energy that is always free to be shared. We cannot expect a truly new way of being to emerge from attempted unions on a biological, emotional, social, economic, or political level. Any union that we form that will really be a *new creation* must be a union of our most characteristic energies, our deepest personal energies. This has been the rule for all the other evolutionary advances to more complex levels of compound being, and we can confidently—if this theory of evolution is valid—expect it to be the rule for us.

But how is an evolutionary advance to a new level of compounded complexity a matter of being "in Christ"? I answer that this way: The Messianic Age is always coming. It is always relative to whatever age of the world we are now in. Life is constantly seeking to renew itself, to transcend itself. The Christ is always the One who was and who is coming. Thus, every age must look forward to the coming of its Messiah, the formative principle that will make all things new. Every age needs to be saved from the deadness of the forms it is on the verge of outgrowing and to be lifted into a new kind of life. Whenever a new creation takes place, it takes place "in Christ."

Each such renewal is a passage to a higher glory, or fuller manifestation, of God. This is the second thing I wish to say about the New Creation. It is an image of the Trinity, a *better* image of the Trinity than previous ones. We frequently say that we are made in the image of God. I want to add that the most significant aspect of this is that we are made in the image of the Trinitarian *perichoresis*: that is, we are *called* to live in that image and can realize our vocation by freely sharing our spondic energies.

Like the Trinity, the New Creation will be simultaneously one and many, both the unity and the multiplicity being generated by the same act, the act of projecting life-giving energies toward fellow members of the community, that is, by *agape* love. This is a very complex relation, for each member of the community is a whole in its own right: this is the importance of retaining and strengthening the reflexivity of the personal consciousness. Each person's sense of self-being is not only fully intact but intensified. It is out of the very intensity and fullness of that sense of transcendent self-being that the agape love springs up and overflows.

Each member is itself a whole, and out of the fullness and intensity of its own sense of wholeness, it radiates life-energy to its fellows. This bonding in turn forms a higher level whole that nevertheless does not destroy or denature the wholeness of the composing members. The bonding by radiation and energy sharing means that each member gives itself in its entirety to each fellow member, so each one's being is fully involved in every other one's being. The consequence of this complex relation is that each member becomes both a permeating energy of the new level whole *and* absolutely unique in its own proper wholeness.

Being absolutely unique, each member is absolutely indispensable to the new level whole. The community cannot afford to lose any one. The community takes the attitude of the shepherd who leaves ninety-nine sheep on the hills and goes to seek the one that is lost. There is no such thing as replacing a person in this community by another individual having the same qualifications.

A major concern of this community, therefore, must be to prize, protect, nurture, and promote each member in that member's unique personhood. Each center of spondic energy in this living Body will realize that it most literally is loving its neighbor as its self and that whatever it does to any member it does to the whole and thereby to every member, including itself.

The New Creation, as a community that images the *perichoresis* of the Trinity, is again Christic, for it is the office of the Christ to manifest God on the earth, to be the presence of God in the midst of the people.

Finally, we come to the third thing I want to say about the new creation, that it is the Living One, the one risen from the dead. I say risen from the dead in the sense of risen *above* the dead, above the dead shells of already formed being, above the dead past. Life is always thrusting into the future. The Living One is found on the edge of tomorrow, participating in the creation of the coming day, for the Living One is also the Creating One.

This is the Christ in the sense of the Logos, the creative Word in which and by which all things come to be. When we are "in Christ" and realize ourselves as the "I am" whose life consists of saying to all beings "May you be," we are active members of this creative activity that makes all things new at every moment. We are the New Creation, not only in the passive sense of being that which is created new, but in the active sense of being those who are participants in the act of creating.

By entering into Christ, the creative Logos, we attain a new level of reflexivity. We become not only the consciousness of consciousness, the self-thinking thought, but the self-creating creature.*

This is probably the most daring and most radical of all the things we can say about the new creation in Christ. If we really accept creation, creation ever new, and if we ourselves are active participants in this ever new creating, then we are always facing the future. We must not seek the Living One among the dead, that is, in the past. This is not to deny that there is continuity with past forms and past patterns. It is to assert that the truly Living One is not found there. The Living One is the one engaged in creating anew, engaged in making the new creation.

If we really accept futurity and the process of continuous creation, it means that the future is really unknown and unknowable. "It has not yet appeared what we shall be." The most general outlines of the structures of the past seem to give us some clues to the forms of the future, but real creativity is not to be found in them. Real creativity

*See Beatrice Bruteau, *God's Ecstasy: The Creation of a Self-Creating World* (New York: Crossroad, 1997).

arises, like the transcendent freedom that empowers it, not as response to the environment, but originally and spontaneously from the heart of the agent as from a first source. If we are to take it seriously, creativity as improvisation becomes a whole philosophical and theological perspective in itself, not reducible to selection and arrangement of materials given in the past.

Creativity may come to be seen as the real interior meaning of the act of faith. The Living One, who is the Creating One, is also the Forgiving One. And forgiveness, as was noted in chapter 8, is an act of faith in the future, a reaching beyond the past and the knowledge of the past into new being, as yet unknown. The act of faith is the act of uniting with the Living One as living, as not dead, as not bound by the past, but as transcendent, free, and creating. It is not an act of knowledge, for knowledge is always of the past. To have faith is to enter into the other's creating, into the other's future, which has not yet appeared.

To enter by our transcendent freedom into Christ and to become a New Creation means to enter by faith into the future of every person and into the very heart of creativity itself, into the future of God.

To be "in Christ" is to accept the offer that Jesus makes, to be food for his friends. As prerequisite to this, one must renounce the lordship pattern of organizing social relations. One must forsake being either dominant or submissive. One must undergo this *metanoia*, this particular mutation in consciousness. To be "in Christ" is to enter into the revolutionary events of Holy Thursday by experiencing the archetypal death and resurrection, letting an old modality of consciousness die and seeing a new one rise to life.

To be "in Christ" is to abandon thinking of oneself only in terms of categories and abstractions by which one may be externally related to others and to coincide with oneself as a transcendent center of energy that lives *in* God and *in* one's fellows—because that is where the Christ lives, in God and in us.

To be "in Christ" is to experience oneself as an initiative of free energy radiating out to give life abundantly to all, for that is the function of the Christ. To be "in Christ" is to be an indispensable member of a living body, which is the Body of Christ. To be "in Christ" is to be identified with the Living One who is not to be sought among the dead, for the Living One is the One who is Coming to Be.

If I am asked, then, "Who do you say I am?" my answer is: "You are the new and ever renewing act of creation. You are all of us, as we are united in You. You are all of us as we live in one another. You are all of us in the whole cosmos as we join in Your exuberant act of creation. You are the Living One who improvises at the frontier of the future; and it has not yet appeared what You shall be."

Index

175

union, 14, 44, 56, 60, 62, 66, 93–94, 102,
    121, 123–34, 136, 140, 143–44,
    155, 169
uniqueness, 61, 77, 94, 96, 102, 122,
    136, 140, 158–59, 170
unity, 51, 94–96, 129, 138, 144, 152–53,
    161, 167–68; complex, 152, 154,
    156; and differentiation, 57–58,
    77, 100, 118–20, 145, 147, 155,
    168, 170, 172–73
universe, 95, 97, 148, 166, 173
unpredictability of the future, 139–40,
    171–73

value, 61–63, 77, 82, 86, 91, 94–97,
    101, 105–6, 109–14, 119, 123,
    132, 138, 145, 152–54, 156,
    170
viability, 99–100

"We," 101, 106, 130, 138, 145, 167
Wei Wu Wei, 115
wholeness, 13, 23, 49, 56, 85–86, 88–89,
    91, 94, 100, 110, 167, 170
wholistic, viii, 59, 87, 95, 100–102,
    119–20, 122–25; consciousness,
    91ff., 93, 96
Wilber, Ken, 126nn.4, 13
will/willingness, 115, 117, 120–21,
    129–30, 136, 139, 140–41, 143, 148
Word, the, 124
worldview, 97–98, 141